EASY WEDDING PLANNING PLUS

CELEBRATING THE WEDDING OF

&

WHO WILL BE MARRIED ON

AT

From America's Top Wedding Experts

Alex & Elizabeth Lluch
Authors of Over 4 Million Books Sold!

WS Publishing Group
San Diego, California

This book is dedicated to brides and grooms everywhere.
May your wedding be one of the happiest days of your lives.

EASY WEDDING PLANNING PLUS

Written by Alex & Elizabeth Lluch
America's Top Wedding Experts

Published by WS Publishing Group
San Diego, California
© Copyright 2014 by WS Publishing Group

Cover photo:
© iStockphoto/kate_sept2004

Special thanks to our contributing photographer:
Karen French
www.karenfrenchphotography.com
Phone: 714.968.5139
Email: info@karenfrenchphotography.com

For inquiries:
Log on to www.WSPublishingGroup.com
Email info@WSPublishingGroup.com

Printed in China

ISBN 13: 978-1-936061-53-2

CONTENTS

GETTING STARTED

❋ Introduction 5
❋ Wedding Events at a Glance 7
❋ Wedding Planning Checklist 11
❋ Budget Analysis. 19
❋ Wedding Consultant 29

CEREMONY & ATTIRE

❋ Ceremony. 33
❋ Unique Wedding Ideas 45
❋ Attire & Beauty 47

PHOTOGRAPHY & VIDEOGRAPHY

❋ Photography 61
❋ Videography 75

STATIONERY & RECEPTION

❋ Stationery. 83
❋ Addressing Invitations 103
❋ Reception. 105

MUSIC & BAKERY

❋ Music 127
❋ Bakery 135

FLOWERS & DECORATIONS

❋ Flowers 141
❋ Decorations. 159

TRANSPORTATION & RENTALS

❋ Transportation 163
❋ Rental Items 167

CONTENTS

GIFTS & PARTIES

❊ Gifts 175

❊ Parties 179

THINGS TO KNOW

❊ Legal Matters. 183

❊ Who Pays for What. 189

❊ Wedding Formations 191

❊ Things to Bring. 197

CALENDAR & TIMELINES

❊ Wedding Planning Calendar 199

❊ Timelines. 209

GREEN WEDDING TIPS

❊ Green Wedding Tips 219

TOP 10 TRENDS, IDEAS & RESOURCES

❊ Top 10 Trends, Ideas & Resources 241

TOP 100 FAQS

❊ Top 100 FAQs 261

HONEYMOON

❊ Honeymoon 279

GETTING STARTED

Peter Morneau
Gown: Justina McCaffrey

INTRODUCTION

DEAR BRIDE AND GROOM,

Congratulations on your engagement! You must be very excited to have found that special person with whom you will share the rest of your life. And you must be looking forward to what will be the happiest day of your life—your wedding! Planning a wedding can be fun and exciting, but it can also be very stressful. That is why WedSpace.com, the top social networking and planning site for weddings, created *Easy Wedding Planning Plus*.

Easy Wedding Planning Plus contains the information you need to plan the wedding of your dreams, keeping you organized every step of the way. Plus, it includes tons of fun and inspirational sections as well!

This book begins with a detailed wedding planning checklist and a comprehensive budget analysis, listing all the expenses that are typically incurred in a wedding. You will also find the percentage of the total budget that is typically spent in each category.

Comparison charts, worksheets, and forms are included in every chapter to help you compare vendors, keep track of important information and appointments, and more. In addition, wedding timelines for your bridal party and your service providers keep everyone on schedule.

We have also included a breakdown of who pays for what, along with the traditional formations for the ceremony, processional, recessional, and receiving line for both Jewish and Christian weddings.

Next, a 9-month calendar helps you keep track of important dates, appointments, meetings, fittings, and much more.

A fun "Top 10" section with lists, such as "Top 10 Wedding Venues," "Top 10 Things to Do with Your Gown Post-Wedding," and "Top 10 Wedding Blogs," will clue you into the latest trends for more inspiration. An FAQ section answers the top 100 most important wedding questions, as seen on WedSpace.com. Green wedding ideas provide the best ways to protect the environment while hosting a beautiful, memorable wedding.

And what about planning the honeymoon of your dreams? A chapter on honeymoons, from choosing the perfect location to creating a packing list, is another great resource.

INTRODUCTION

Let this book be your complete wedding guide and organizer before, during, and after your wedding! We are confident you will enjoy planning your wedding with the help of *Easy Wedding Planning Plus*. If you can think of anything else you would like to see included in a future edition of this book, please write to us at: WS Publishing Group, Inc., 15373 Innovation Drive Suite #360, San Diego, CA 92128. We will include your ideas and suggestions in our next printing. We listen to brides and grooms like you—that's why we have become the best-selling publisher of wedding planners!

Sincerely,

Elizabeth H. Lluch

WEDDING EVENTS
AT A GLANCE

YOUR WEDDING WILL BE A CELEBRATION that will most likely span over several different events. From the moment you get engaged, to your last dance, to your honeymoon, there will be much to plan and do.

Use the following worksheets to easily keep track of events, dates, locations, and contact information. Keeping these details in one place will help you plan ahead for each party and quickly reference important information.

Once you have finalized all of your events, make copies of these worksheets and distribute them to the members of your wedding party, consultants, or vendors who require this information.

WEDDING EVENTS AT A GLANCE

ENGAGEMENT PARTY DATE: N/A

Engagement Party Time:

Engagement Party Location:

Contact Person: Phone Number:

Website: Email:

BRIDAL SHOWER DATE:

Bridal Shower Time:

Bridal Shower Location:

Contact Person: Phone Number:

Website: Email:

BACHELOR PARTY DATE:

Bachelor Party Time:

Bachelor Party Location:

Contact Person: Phone Number:

Website: Email:

BACHELORETTE PARTY DATE:

Bachelorette Party Time:

Bachelorette Party Location:

Contact Person: Phone Number:

Website: Email:

CEREMONY REHEARSAL DATE: 5/25/18

Ceremony Rehearsal Time:

Ceremony Rehearsal Location: Seabrook

Contact Person: Phone Number:

Website: Email:

REHEARSAL DINNER DATE: 5/25/18

Rehearsal Dinner Time:

Rehearsal Dinner Location:

Contact Person: Phone Number:

Website: Email:

CEREMONY DATE: 5/26/18

Ceremony Time:

Ceremony Location:

Contact Person: Phone Number:

Website: Email:

RECEPTION DATE: 5/26/18

Reception Time:

Reception Location:

Contact Person: Phone Number:

Website: Email:

2:30 - 8:30 Warehouse
11:30 - 2:30 Church

INFORMATION AT A GLANCE

VENDOR	Company	Contact Person	Phone #	Website/Email
Wedding Consultant	Day Dream	Daylee Howard		
Ceremony Site	St. Joseph's Church			
Officiant	Fr Gary Lazzeroni			
Reception Site	Warehouse 23	Sunny Golden	360·726·6583	
Caterer	{	{	{	
Liquor Services	↓	↓	↓	
Wedding Gown				
Tuxedo Rental	Mens Warehouse			
Photographer		Stefani Rose		
Videographer				
Stationer				
Calligrapher				
Music: Ceremony	David Bentz & Karl Rhodes			
Music: Reception	Family Friendly DJ, LLC	David Child	360-991-6665	
Florist		Mandi Nelson		
Bakery	Simply Sweets	Tasha	360-896-7321	
Decorations	Hailey			
Ice Sculpture				
Party Favor	Hailey			
Transportation	Byron to arrange.			
Rental & Supplies	N/A			
Gift Suppliers				
Valet Services	Homewood Suites			
Gift Attendant				
Rehearsal Dinner				
Wedding Website	Wedding Wire			

WEDDING PLANNING CHECKLIST

THE FOLLOWING WEDDING PLANNING CHECKLIST ITEMIZES everything you need to do or consider when planning your wedding, along with the best time frame in which to accomplish each activity.

This checklist assumes that you have at least nine months to plan your wedding. If your wedding is sooner, just start at the beginning of the list and catch up as quickly as you can!

Use the boxes to the left of the items to check off the activities as you accomplish them. This will enable you to see your progress, as well as help you determine what has been done, and what still needs to be done.

Note: This book uses the traditional term, "usher," to describe those performing the duties of groomsmen. However, some couples today opt to separate groomsmen and ushers into two different groups performing varying duties. Keep this in mind when planning your own wedding party.

-Tell family what colors to wear.

NINE MONTHS AND EARLIER

- ☑ Announce your engagement.

- ☑ Select a date for your wedding.

- ☑ Hire a professional wedding consultant. *Maybe... Daylee Howard*

- ☑ Determine the type of wedding you want: location, formality, time of day, number of guests.

- ☑ Determine budget and how expenses will be shared.

- ☑ Develop a record-keeping system for payments made.

- ☑ Consolidate all guest lists: bride's list, groom's list, bride's family list, groom's family list, and organize:
    1) those who must be invited
    2) those who should be invited
    3) those who it would be nice to invite

- ☑ Decide if you want to include children among guests.

- ☑ Select and reserve ceremony site.

- ☑ Select and reserve your officiant.

NINE MONTHS AND EARLIER (CONT'D)

- ☑ Select and reserve reception site.

- ☑ Select and order your bridal gown and headpiece.

- ☑ Determine color scheme.

- ☐ Use the calendar provided to note all important activities: showers, luncheons, parties, get-togethers, etc.

- ☐ If ceremony or reception is at *N/A* home, arrange for home or garden improvements as needed.

- ☑ Select and <u>book</u> photographer.

- ☐ Order passport, visa, or birth certificate, if needed, for your marriage license or honeymoon.

- ☑ Select maid of honor, best man, bridesmaids, and ushers (approximately one usher per 50 guests).

SIX TO NINE MONTHS BEFORE WEDDING

☑ Select flower girl and ring bearer.

❑ Give the *Wedding Party Responsibility Cards* to your wedding party. These cards are published by WS Publishing Group and are available at major bookstores. *What?*

❑ Reserve wedding night bridal suite.

☑ Select attendants' dresses, shoes, and accessories. *Need mens attire.*

☑ Select and book caterer, if needed.

☑ Select and book ceremony musicians. *Karl* *Kenissa will help w/this.*

☑ Select and book reception musicians or DJ.

☑ Schedule fittings and delivery dates for yourself, attendants, and flower girl.

❑ Select and book videographer. *N/A*

☑ Select and book florist.
Need contract from florist.

FOUR TO SIX MONTHS BEFORE WEDDING

❑ Start shopping for each other's wedding gifts.

☑ Reserve rental items needed for ceremony.

☑ Finalize guest list.

❑ Select and order wedding invitations, announcements, and other stationery, such as thank you notes, wedding programs, and seating cards.

❑ Address invitations or hire a calligrapher.

☑ Set date, time, and location for your rehearsal dinner.

☑ Arrange accommodations for out-of-town guests.

☑ Start planning your honeymoon.

❑ Select and book all miscellaneous *N/A* services, i.e. gift attendant, valet parking, etc.

☑ Register for gifts. *will need to modify.*

☑ Purchase shoes and accessories.

☑ Begin to break in your shoes.

WEDDING PLANNING CHECKLIST

TWO TO FOUR MONTHS BEFORE WEDDING

- ✓ Select bakery and order wedding cake.

- ☐ Order party favors. *N/A*

- ☐ Select and order room decorations. *N/A*

- ☐ Purchase honeymoon
  attire and luggage.

- ☐ Select and book transportation
  for wedding day.

- ✓ Check marriage
  license requirements.

- ☐ Shop for wedding rings and
  have them engraved.

- ☐ Consider having your teeth
  cleaned or bleached. *N/A*

- ☐ Consider writing a will and/or
  prenuptial agreement. *After wedding Maybe*

- ☐ Plan activities for out-of-town guests,
  both before and after the wedding.

- ☐ Purchase gifts for wedding attendants.

SIX TO EIGHT WEEKS BEFORE WEDDING

- ☐ Mail invitations. Include
  accommodation choices and a
  map to assist guests in finding
  the ceremony and reception sites.

- ✓ Maintain a record of RSVPs and all
  gifts received. Send thank you notes
  upon receipt of gifts.

- ✓ Determine hairstyle and makeup.

- ☐ Schedule to have your hair,
  makeup, and nails done the day
  of the wedding.

- ☐ Finalize shopping for wedding day
  accessories such as toasting glasses,
  ring pillow, guest book, etc.

- ✓ Set up an area or a table in your home
  to display gifts as you receive them. *@ reception.*

- ☐ Check with your local newspapers for
  wedding announcement requirements. *N/A.*

- ☐ Have your formal bridal
  portrait taken. *N/A*

- ☐ Send wedding announcement and
  photograph to your local newspapers. *N/A*

SIX TO EIGHT WEEKS BEFORE WEDDING (CONT'D)

❑ Check requirements to change your name and address on your driver's license, social security card, insurance policies, subscriptions, bank accounts, etc.

— Hailey only.

❑ Select and reserve wedding attire for groom, ushers, ring bearer, and father of the bride.

❑ Select a guest book attendant. Decide where and when to have guests sign in.

Reception. MoH can manage?

❑ Mail invitations to rehearsal dinner.

❑ Obtain marriage license.

❑ Plan a luncheon or dinner with your bridesmaids. Give them their gifts at that time or at the rehearsal dinner.

N/A ✓ ✓

❑ Find "something old, something new, something borrowed, something blue, and a sixpence (or shiny penny) for your shoe."

✓ Finalize your menu, beverage, and alcohol order.

TWO TO SIX WEEKS BEFORE WEDDING

❑ Confirm ceremony details with your officiant.

✓ Arrange final fitting of bridesmaids' dresses.

✓ Have final fitting of your gown and headpiece.

✓ Make final floral selections.

❑ Finalize rehearsal dinner plans; arrange seating and write names on place cards if desired.

❑ Make a detailed timeline for your wedding party.

❑ Make a detailed timeline for your service providers.

Planner

❑ Confirm details with all service providers, including attire. Give them copies of your wedding timeline. *Planner to do this?*

❑ Start packing for your honeymoon.

❑ Finalize addressing and stamping announcements.

❑ Contact guests who haven't responded.

TWO TO SIX WEEKS BEFORE WEDDING (CONT'D)

❑ Decide if you want to form a receiving line. If so, determine when and where to form the line.
No... @ reception.

❑ Pick up rings and check for fit.

❑ Meet with photographer and confirm special photos you want taken.

❑ Meet with videographer and confirm special events or people you want filmed. *N/A*

❑ Meet with musicians and confirm music to be played during special events, such as the first dance.

❑ Continue writing thank you notes as gifts arrive.

❑ Remind bridesmaids and ushers of when and where to pick up their wedding attire.

❑ Purchase the lipstick, nail polish, and any other accessories you want your bridesmaids to wear.

❑ Determine ceremony seating for special guests. Give a list to the ushers.

❑ Plan reception room layout and seating with your site manager or caterer. Write names on place cards for arranged seating.

THE LAST WEEK

❑ Pick up wedding attire and make sure everything fits.

❑ Do final guest count and notify your caterer or reception site manager.

❑ Gather everything you will need for the rehearsal and wedding day as listed in the *Wedding Party Responsibility Cards*.

❑ Arrange for someone to drive the getaway car.

❑ Review the schedule of events and last minute arrangements with your service providers. Give them each a detailed timeline.

❑ Confirm all honeymoon reservations and accommodations. Pick up tickets and travelers checks.

❑ Finish packing your suitcases for the honeymoon.

❑ Familiarize yourself with guests' names. It will help during the receiving line and reception.

❑ Notify the post office to hold mail while you are away on your honeymoon.

THE REHEARSAL DAY

- ❏ Review list of things to bring to the rehearsal provided in this book.

- ❏ Put suitcases in getaway car.

- ❏ Give your bridesmaids the lipstick, nail polish, and accessories you want them to wear for the wedding.

- ❏ Give best man the officiant's fee and any other checks for service providers. Instruct him to deliver these checks the day of the wedding.

- ❏ Arrange for someone to bring accessories such as flower basket, ring pillow, guest book and pen, toasting glasses, cake cutting knife, and napkins to the ceremony and reception.

- ❏ Arrange for someone to mail announcements the day after the wedding.

- ❏ Arrange for someone to return rental items such as tuxedos, slip, and cake pillars after the wedding.

- ❏ Provide each member of your wedding party with a detailed schedule of events/timelines for the wedding day.

- ❏ Review ceremony seating with ushers.

THE WEDDING DAY

- ❏ Review list of things to bring to the ceremony provided in this book.

- ❏ Give the groom's ring to the maid of honor.

- ❏ Give the bride's ring to the best man.

- ❏ Simply follow your detailed schedule of events.

- ❏ Relax and enjoy your wedding!

NOTES

BUDGET ANALYSIS

THIS COMPREHENSIVE BUDGET ANALYSIS HAS BEEN DESIGNED to provide you with all the expenses that can be incurred in any size wedding, including hidden costs, such as taxes, gratuities, stamps, and other items that can easily add up to thousands of dollars in a wedding. After you have completed this budget, you will have a much better idea of what your wedding will cost. You can then prioritize and allocate your money accordingly.

This budget is divided into fifteen categories: Ceremony, Wedding Attire, Photography, Videography, Stationery, Reception, Music, Bakery, Flowers, Decorations, Transportation, Rental Items, Gifts, Parties, and Miscellaneous.

The beginning of each category showcases the percentage of a total wedding budget that is typically spent in that category, based on national averages. Multiply your intended wedding budget by this percentage, and write that amount in the "Budget" space provided.

To determine the total cost of your wedding, estimate the amount of money you will spend on each item in the budget analysis, and write that amount in the "Budget" column after each item. Items printed in italics are traditionally paid for by the groom or his family.

Add all the "Budget" amounts within each category, and write the total amount in the "Subtotal" space at the end of each category. Then add all the "Subtotal" figures to come up with your final wedding budget. The "Actual" column is for you to input your actual expenses as you purchase items or hire your service providers. Writing down the actual expenses will help you stay within your budget.

For example, if your total wedding budget is $20,000, write this amount at the top of your budget worksheet. To figure your typical ceremony expenses, multiply $20,000 by .05 (5%) to get $1,000. Write this amount on the "Budget" line in the "Ceremony" category to serve as a guide for all your ceremony expenses.

If you find that the total amount is more than what you wanted to spend after adding up all your "Subtotals," simply decide which items are more important to you, and adjust your expenses accordingly.

CHECKLIST OF BUDGET ITEMS

CEREMONY

- ❑ Ceremony Site Fee
- ❑ *Officiant's Fee*
- ❑ *Officiant's Gratuity*
- ❑ Guest Book/Pen/Penholder
- ❑ Ring Bearer Pillow
- ❑ Flower Girl Basket

WEDDING ATTIRE

- ❑ Bridal Gown
- ❑ Alterations
- ❑ Headpiece/Veil
- ☑ Gloves
- ❑ Jewelry
- ❑ Garter/Stockings
- ❑ Shoes
- ❑ Hairdresser
- ☑ Makeup Artist
- ❑ Manicure/Pedicure
- ❑ *Groom's Formal Wear*

PHOTOGRAPHY

- ❑ Bride & Groom's Album
- ❑ Engagement Photographs
- ❑ Formal Bridal Portrait
- ❑ Parents' Album
- ❑ Proofs/Previews
- ❑ Digital Files
- ❑ Extra Prints

VIDEOGRAPHY

- ❑ Main Video
- ☑ Titles
- ☑ Extra Hours
- ☑ Photo Montage
- ☑ Extra Copies

STATIONERY

- ❑ Invitations
- ❑ Response Cards
- ❑ Reception Cards
- ❑ Ceremony Cards
- ☑ Pew Cards
- ☑ Seating/Place Cards
- ❑ Rain Cards
- ☑ Maps
- ☑ Ceremony Programs
- ❑ Announcements
- ❑ Thank You Notes
- ❑ Stamps
- ☑ Calligraphy
- ☑ Napkins/Matchbooks

RECEPTION

- ❑ Reception Site Fee
- ❑ Hors d'Oeuvres
- ❑ Main Meal/Caterer
- ❑ Liquor/Beverages
- ❑ Bartending/Bar Setup Fee
- ❑ Corkage Fee
- ❑ Fee to Pour Coffee

RECEPTION (CONT'D)

- ❑ Service Providers' Meals
- ❑ Gratuity
- ❑ Party Favors
- ☑ Disposable Cameras
- ❑ Rose Petals/Rice
- ☑ Gift Attendant
- ☑ Parking Fee/Valet Services

MUSIC

- ❑ Ceremony Music
- ❑ Reception Music

BAKERY

- ❑ Wedding Cake
- ☑ *Groom's Cake*
- ❑ Cake Delivery/Setup Fee
- ❑ Cake Cutting Fee
- ❑ Cake Topper
- ❑ Cake Knife/Toasting Glasses

FLOWERS

BOUQUETS
- ❑ *Bride*
- ❑ Tossing
- ❑ Maid of Honor
- ❑ Bridesmaid

Items in italics are traditionally paid for by the groom or his family.

FLOWERS (CONT'D)

FLORAL HAIRPIECES
- ☑ Maid of Honor/Bridesmaids
- ☑ Flower Girl

CORSAGES
- ☑ *Bride's Going Away*
- ❏ *Family Members*

BOUTONNIERES
- ❏ *Groom*
- ❏ *Ushers/Other Family Members*

CEREMONY SITE
- ❏ Main Altar
- ❏ Altar Candelabra
- ❏ Aisle Pews

RECEPTION SITE
- ❏ Head Table
- ❏ Guest Tables
- ❏ Buffet Table
- ❏ Punch Table
- ❏ Cake Table
- ❏ Cake
- ❏ Cake Knife
- ❏ Toasting Glasses
- ❏ Floral Delivery/Setup Fee

DECORATIONS

- ❏ Detailed Decorations
- ❏ Table Centerpieces

TRANSPORTATION

- ❏ Transportation

RENTAL ITEMS

- ❏ Bridal Slip
- ❏ Ceremony Accessories
- ❏ Tent/Canopy
- ❏ Dance Floor
- ❏ Tables/Chairs
- ❏ Linen/Tableware
- ❏ Heaters
- ❏ Lanterns
- ❏ Other Rental Items

GIFTS

- ❏ *Bride's Gift*
- ❏ Groom's Gift
- ❏ Bridesmaids' Gifts
- ❏ *Ushers' Gifts*

PARTIES

- ☑ Engagement Party
- ☑ Bridesmaids' Luncheon
- ❏ Bridal Shower
- ❏ *Bachelor Party*
- ❏ Bachelorette Party
- ❏ *Rehearsal Dinner*
- ❏ Day-After Brunch

MISCELLANEOUS

- ❏ Newspaper Announcements
- ❏ *Marriage License*
- ☑ *Prenuptial Agreement*
- ❏ Bridal Gown Preservation
- ❏ Bridal Bouquet Preservation
- ❏ Wedding Consultant
- ❏ Wedding Planning Online
- ❏ Taxes

Items in italics are traditionally paid for by the groom or his family.

BUDGET ANALYSIS

Deposit: $718.08

WEDDING BUDGET	Budget	Actual
YOUR TOTAL WEDDING BUDGET	$ 7,000.00	$
CEREMONY (Typically = 5% of Budget)	$	$
Ceremony Site Fee	$2393.00	$
Officiant's Fee	$	$
Officiant's Gratuity	$	$
Guest Book/Pen/Penholder	$	$
Ring Bearer Pillow	$	$
Flower Girl Basket	$	$
SUBTOTAL 1	$	$

WEDDING ATTIRE (Typically = 10% of Budget)	Budget	Actual
WEDDING ATTIRE (Typically = 10% of Budget)	$	$
Bridal Gown	$	$
Alterations	$	$
Headpiece/Veil	$	$
Gloves	$	$
Jewelry	$	$
Garter/Stockings	$	$
Shoes	$	$
Hairdresser	$	$
Makeup Artist	$	$
Manicure/Pedicure	$	$
Groom's Formal Wear	$	$
SUBTOTAL 2	$	$

PHOTOGRAPHY (Typically = 9% of Budget)	Budget	Actual
PHOTOGRAPHY (Typically = 9% of Budget)	$2000.00	$
Bride & Groom's Album	$	$
Engagement Photographs	$ 400—	$ 400.00
Formal Bridal Portrait	$	$
Parents' Album	$	$
Proofs/Previews	$	$

Items in italics are traditionally paid for by the groom or his family.

WEDDING BUDGET	Budget	Actual
PHOTOGRAPHY (CONT'D)	$	$
Digital Files	$	$
Extra Prints	$	$
SUBTOTAL 3	$	$

VIDEOGRAPHY (Typically = 5% of Budget)	Budget	Actual
	$	$
Main Video	$	$
Titles	$	$
Extra Hours	$	$
Photo Montage	$	$
Extra Copies	$	$
SUBTOTAL 4	$	$

STATIONERY (Typically = 4% of Budget)	Budget	Actual
	$	$
Invitations	$	$
Response Cards	$	$
Reception Cards	$	$
Ceremony Cards	$	$
Pew Cards	$	$
Seating/Place Cards	$	$
Rain Cards	$	$
Maps	$	$
Ceremony Programs	$	$
Announcements	$	$
Thank You Notes	$	$
Stamps	$	$
Calligraphy	$	$
Napkins/Matchbooks	$	$
SUBTOTAL 5	$	$

Items in italics are traditionally paid for by the groom or his family.

WEDDING BUDGET	Budget	Actual
RECEPTION (Typically = 35% of Budget)	$	$
Reception Site Fee	$ *Included w/Ceremony!*	$
Hors d'Oeuvres	$ 250.00	$
Main Meal/Caterer	$ 2,000	$
Liquor/Beverages	$ 1,000	$
Bartending/Bar Setup Fee	$	$
Corkage Fee	$	$
Fee to Pour Coffee	$	$
Service Providers' Meals	$	$
Gratuity	$	$
Party Favors	$	$
Disposable Cameras	$	$
Rose Petals/Rice	$	$
Gift Attendant	$	$
Parking Fee/Valet Services	$	$
SUBTOTAL 6	$	$

Ask! ↕

	Budget	Actual
MUSIC (Typically = 5% of Budget)	$	$
Ceremony Music	$	$
Reception Music	$	$
SUBTOTAL 7	$	$

	Budget	Actual
BAKERY (Typically = 2% of Budget)	$	$
Wedding Cake	$	$
Groom's Cake	$	$
Cake Delivery/Setup Fee	$	$
Cake Cutting Fee	$	$
Cake Topper	$	$
Cake Knife/Toasting Glasses	$	$
SUBTOTAL 8	$	$

Items in italics are traditionally paid for by the groom or his family.

WEDGING BUDGET	Budget	Actual
FLOWERS (Typically = 6% of Budget)	$	$
BOUQUETS	$	$
Bride	$	$
Tossing	$	$
Maid of Honor	$	$
Bridesmaids	$	$
FLORAL HAIRPIECES	$	$
Maid of Honor/Bridesmaids	$	$
Flower Girl	$	$
CORSAGES	$	$
Bride's Going Away	$	$
Family Members	$	$
BOUTONNIERES	$	$
Groom	$	$
Ushers/Other Family Members	$	$
CEREMONY SITE	$	$
Main Altar	$	$
Altar Candelabra	$	$
Aisle Pews	$	$
RECEPTION SITE	$	$
Reception Site	$	$
Head Table	$	$
Guest Tables	$	$
Buffet Table	$	$
Punch Table	$	$
Cake Table	$	$
Cake	$	$
Cake Knife	$	$
Toasting Glasses	$	$
Floral Delivery/Setup Fee	$	$
SUBTOTAL 9	$	$

Items in italics are traditionally paid for by the groom or his family.

WEDDING BUDGET	Budget	Actual
DECORATIONS (Typically = 3% of Budget)	$	$
Detailed Decorations	$	$
Table Centerpieces	$	$
SUBTOTAL 10	$	$

TRANSPORTATION (Typically = 2% of Budget)	$	$
Transportation	$	$
SUBTOTAL 11	$	$

RENTAL ITEMS (Typically = 3% of Budget)	$	$
Bridal Slip	$	$
Ceremony Accessories	$	$
Tent/Canopy	$	$
Dance Floor	$	$
Tables/Chairs	$	$
Linen/Tableware	$	$
Heaters	$	$
Lanterns	$	$
Other Rental Items	$	$
SUBTOTAL 12	$	$

GIFTS (Typically = 3% of Budget)	$	$
Bride's Gift	$	$
Groom's Gift	$	$
Bridesmaids' Gifts	$	$
Ushers' Gifts	$	$
SUBTOTAL 13	$	$

Items in italics are traditionally paid for by the groom or his family.

WEDDING BUDGET	Budget	Actual
PARTIES (Typically = 4% of Budget)	$	$
Engagement Party	$	$
Bridal Shower	$	$
Bachelor Party	$	$
Bachelorette Party	$	$
Bridesmaids' Luncheon	$	$
Rehearsal Dinner	$	$
Day-After Brunch	$	$
SUBTOTAL 14	$	$

MISCELLANEOUS (Typically = 4% of Budget)	Budget	Actual
MISCELLANEOUS (Typically = 4% of Budget)	$	$
Newspaper Announcements	$	$
Marriage License	$	$
Prenuptial Agreement	$	$
Bridal Gown Preservation	$	$
Bridal Bouquet Preservation	$	$
Wedding Consultant	$	$
Online Wedding Planning	$	$
Taxes	$	$
SUBTOTAL 15	$	$

	Budget	Actual
GRAND TOTAL (Add "Budget" & "Actual" Subtotals 1-15)	$	$

Items in italics are traditionally paid for by the groom or his family.

VENDOR PAYMENT TRACKING CHART

VENDOR	Business Name & Phone Number	Website & Email Address	Contract Date & Total Cost	Deposit & Date	Next Pymt. & Date	Final Pymt. & Date
Wedding Consultant						
Ceremony Site						
Officiant						
Reception Site						
Caterer						
Liquor Services						
Wedding Gown						
Tuxedo Rental						
Photographer						
Videographer						
Stationer						
Calligrapher						
Music: Ceremony						
Music: Reception						
Florist						
Bakery						
Decorations						
Ice Sculpture						
Party Favors						
Transportation						
Rental & Supplies						
Gift Suppliers						
Valet Services						
Gift Attendant						
Rehearsal Dinner						
Wedding Website						

WEDDING CONSULTANT

WEDDING CONSULTANTS ARE PROFESSIONALS whose training, expertise, and contacts will help make your wedding as close to perfect as possible. They can save you considerable time, money, and stress when planning your wedding.

Contrary to what many people believe, a wedding consultant is part of your wedding budget, not an extra expense! Wedding consultants have information on many ceremony and reception sites, as well as reliable service providers, which will save you hours of investigation and legwork.

Options: A consultant can help you plan the whole event from beginning to end, assisting you in formulating a budget, along with selecting your ceremony and reception sites, flowers, invitations, and service providers.

Or, a wedding consultant can simply help coordinate the rehearsal and the wedding day. Remember, you want to feel like a guest at your own wedding. You and your family should not have to worry about any details on that special day. That is the wedding consultant's job!

You can have a wedding consultant help you do as much or as little as you think necessary.

Things to Consider: Wedding consultants can save you stress by ensuring that what you are planning is correct, and that the service providers you hire are reliable and professional. Most service providers recommended by wedding consultants will go out of their way to do an excellent job for you so that the wedding consultant will continue to recommend their services.

Tips to Save Money: A good wedding consultant should be able to save you at least the amount of his or her fee by suggesting less expensive alternatives that still enhance your wedding, or by obtaining discounts from the service providers. If this isn't enough, they are more than worth their fee by serving as an intermediary between you, your parents, and your service providers.

Price Range: $500 to $10,000

WEDDING CONSULTANT COMPARISON CHART

QUESTIONS	POSSIBILITY 1	POSSIBILITY 2
What is the name of the wedding consulting business?		
What is the website and email of the wedding consultant?		
What is the address of the wedding consultant?		
What is the phone number of the wedding consultant?		
How many years of professional experience do you have?		
How many consultants are in your company?		
Are you a member of the Association of Bridal Consultants?		
What services do you provide?		
What are your hourly fees?		
What is your fee for complete wedding planning?		
What is your fee to oversee the rehearsal and wedding day?		
What is your payment policy?		
What is your cancellation policy?		
Do you have liability insurance?		

POSSIBILITY 3	POSSIBILITY 4	POSSIBILITY 5	POSSIBILITY 6

WEDDING CONSULTANT'S INFORMATION FORM

Make a copy of this form and give it to your wedding consultant.

THE WEDDING OF:

Ceremony Site: _____ Phone Number: _____

Ceremony Address: _____

City: _____ State: _____ Zip Code: _____

Website: _____ Email: _____

Reception Site: _____ Phone Number: _____

Reception Address: _____

City: _____ State: _____ Zip Code: _____

Website: _____ Email: _____

CEREMONY SERVICES	Contact Person	Arrival Time	Departure Time	Phone Number
Florist				
Musicians				
Officiant				
Photographer				
Rental Supplier				
Site Coordinator				
Soloist				
Transportation				
Videographer				

RECEPTION SERVICES	Contact Person	Arrival Time	Departure Time	Phone Number
Baker				
Bartender				
Caterer				
Florist				
Gift Attendant				
Guest Book Attendant				
Musicians				
Rental Supplier				
Site Coordinator				
Transportation				
Valet Service				

CEREMONY & ATTIRE

Karen French

KAREN FRENCH

KAREN FRENCH

KAREN FRENCH

KAREN FRENCH

KAREN FRENCH

CEREMONY

YOUR CEREMONY IS A REFLECTION OF WHO YOU ARE. It can be as simple or as elaborate as you desire. Many people choose to have a traditional ceremony in a church, while others have taken their special day outdoors to a park or the beach. These days, anything goes!

CEREMONY SITE FEE

The ceremony site fee is the fee to rent a facility for your wedding. In churches, cathedrals, chapels, temples, or synagogues, this fee may include the organist, wedding coordinator, custodian, changing rooms for the bridal party, and miscellaneous items such as kneeling cushions, an aisle runner, and a candelabra. Be sure to ask what the site fee includes prior to booking a facility. Throughout this book, the word church will be used to refer to the site where the ceremony will take place.

Options: Churches, cathedrals, chapels, temples, synagogues, private homes, gardens, hotels, clubs, halls, parks, museums, yachts, wineries, beaches, and hot air balloons.

Things to Consider: Your selection of a ceremony site will be influenced by the formality of your wedding, the season of the year, the number of guests expected, and your religious affiliation. Make sure you ask about restrictions or guidelines regarding photography, videography, music, decorations, candles, and rice or rose petal tossing. Consider issues such as proximity of the ceremony site to the recep-

tion site, parking availability, handicapped accessibility, and time constraints.

Tips to Save Money: Have your ceremony at the same facility as your reception to save a second rental fee. Set a realistic guest list and stick to it. Hire an experienced wedding consultant to help you find the best rates. At a church or temple, ask if there is another wedding that day and share the cost of floral decorations with that bride. At a garden wedding, have guests stand to omit the cost of renting chairs. Additionally, membership in a church, temple, or club can reduce rental fees.

Price Range: $100 - $1,000

OFFICIANT'S FEE

The officiant's fee is the fee paid to the person who performs your wedding ceremony.

Options: Priest, Clergyman, Minister, Pastor, Chaplain, Rabbi, Judge, or Justice of the Peace. These days, it is also popular to have a friend or family member of the couple perform the marriage ceremony after becoming ordained through quick and inexpensive online programs. Having someone special perform the ceremony that will bind you and your partner for life can make your wedding even more meaningful.

Discuss the readings you would like incorporated into your ceremony with your officiant. Some popular readings include:

Beatitudes	Corinthians 13:1-13	Ecclesiastes 3:1-9
Ephesians 3:14-19; 5:1-2	Genesis 1:26-28	Genesis 2:4-9, 15-24
Hosea 2:19-21	Isaiah 61:10-62:3	John 4:7-16
John 15:9-12, 17:22-24	Mark 10:6-9	Proverbs 31:10-31
Romans 12:1-2, 9-18	Ruth 1:16-17	Tobit 8:56-58

Things to Consider: Some officiants may not accept a fee, depending on your relationship with him or her. If a fee is refused, send a donation to the officiant's church or synagogue.

Price Range: $100 - $500

OFFICIANT'S GRATUITY

The officiant's gratuity is a discretionary amount of money given to the officiant.

Things to Consider: This amount should depend on your relationship with the officiant and the amount of time he or she has spent with you prior to the ceremony. The groom puts the gratuity in a sealed envelope and gives it to his best man or wedding consultant, who, in turn, gives it to the officiant either before or immediately after the ceremony.

Price Range: $50 - $250

GUEST BOOK/PEN/PENHOLDER

The guest book is a formal register that your guests sign as they arrive at the ceremony or reception. It serves as a memento displaying who attended your wedding. This book is often placed outside the ceremony or reception site, along with an elegant pen and penholder. A guest book attendant is responsible for inviting all guests to sign in. A younger sibling or close friend who is not a part of the wedding party may be well-suited for this position.

Options: There are many styles of guest books, pens, and penholders to choose from. Some books have space for your guests to write a short note to the bride and groom.

Things to Consider: Make sure you have more than one pen in case one runs out of ink. If you are planning a large ceremony (over 300 guests), consider having more than one book and pen so that your guests don't have to wait in line to sign it.

Price Range: $30 - $100

RING BEARER PILLOW

The ring bearer, usually a boy between the ages of four and eight, carries the bride and groom's rings or mock rings on a pillow. He follows the maid of honor and precedes the flower girl or bride in the processional.

Options: These pillows come in many styles and colors. You can find them at most gift shops and bridal boutiques.

Things to Consider: If the ring bearer is very young (less than 7 years), place mock rings on the pillow in place of the real rings to prevent losing them. If mock rings are used, instruct your ring bearer to put the pillow upside down during the recessional so your guests don't see them.

Tips to Save Money: Make your own ring bearer pillow by taking a small white pillow and attaching a pretty ribbon to it to hold the rings.

Price Range: $15 - $75

FLOWER GIRL BASKET

The flower girl, usually between the ages of four and eight, carries a basket filled with flowers, rose petals, or paper rose petals to scatter as she walks down the aisle. She follows the ring bearer or maid of honor and precedes the bride during the processional.

Options: Flower girl baskets come in many styles and colors. You can find them at most florists, gift shops, and bridal boutiques.

Things to Consider: Discuss any restrictions regarding rose petal, flower, or paper-tossing with your ceremony site. Select a basket which complements your guest book and ring bearer pillow. If the flower girl is very young (less than 7 years), consider giving her a small bouquet instead of a flower basket.

Tips to Save Money: Ask your florist if you can borrow a basket and attach a pretty white bow to it.

Price Range: $20 - $75

CEREMONY SITE COMPARISON CHART

QUESTIONS	POSSIBILITY 1	POSSIBILITY 2
What is the name of the ceremony site?		
What is the website and email of the ceremony site?		
What is the address of the ceremony site?		
What is the name and phone number of my contact person?		
What dates and times are available?		
Do vows need to be approved?		
What is the ceremony site fee?		
What is the payment policy?		
What is the cancellation policy?		
Does the facility have liability insurance?		
What are the minimum/maximum number of guests allowed?		
What is the denomination, if any, of the facility?		
What restrictions are there with regards to religion?		
Is an officiant available? At what cost?		
Are outside officiants allowed?		
Are any musical instruments available for our use?		
If so, what is the fee?		

POSSIBILITY 3	POSSIBILITY 4	POSSIBILITY 5	POSSIBILITY 6

CEREMONY SITE COMPARISON CHART (CONT'D)

QUESTIONS	POSSIBILITY 1	POSSIBILITY 2
What music restrictions are there, if any?		
What photography restrictions are there, if any?		
What videography restrictions are there, if any?		
Are there any restrictions for rice/petal tossing ?		
Are candlelight ceremonies allowed?		
What floral decorations are available/allowed?		
When is my rehearsal to be scheduled?		
Is there handicap accessibility and parking?		
How many parking spaces are available for my wedding party?		
Where are they located?		
How many parking spaces are available for my guests?		
What rental items are necessary?		
What is the fee?		

POSSIBILITY 3	POSSIBILITY 4	POSSIBILITY 5	POSSIBILITY 6

PEW SEATING ARRANGEMENTS

Complete this form only after finalizing your guest list.

BRIDE'S FAMILY SECTION

• PEW _____

_____
_____
_____
_____
_____
_____
_____
_____
_____

• PEW _____

_____
_____
_____
_____
_____
_____
_____
_____
_____

• PEW _____

_____
_____
_____
_____
_____
_____
_____
_____
_____

• PEW _____

_____
_____
_____
_____
_____
_____
_____
_____
_____

• PEW _____

_____
_____
_____
_____
_____
_____
_____
_____
_____

• PEW _____

_____
_____
_____
_____
_____
_____
_____
_____
_____

• PEW _____

_____
_____
_____
_____
_____
_____
_____
_____
_____

• PEW _____

_____
_____
_____
_____
_____
_____
_____
_____
_____

• PEW _____

_____
_____
_____
_____
_____
_____
_____
_____
_____

PEW SEATING ARRANGEMENTS

Complete this form only after finalizing your guest list.

GROOM'S FAMILY SECTION

• PEW _____

_____
_____
_____
_____
_____
_____
_____
_____

• PEW _____

_____
_____
_____
_____
_____
_____
_____
_____
_____
_____

• PEW _____

_____
_____
_____
_____
_____
_____
_____
_____
_____
_____

• PEW _____

_____
_____
_____
_____
_____
_____
_____
_____
_____
_____

• PEW _____

_____
_____
_____
_____
_____
_____
_____
_____
_____
_____

• PEW _____

_____
_____
_____
_____
_____
_____
_____
_____
_____
_____

• PEW _____

_____
_____
_____
_____
_____
_____
_____
_____
_____
_____

• PEW _____

_____
_____
_____
_____
_____
_____
_____
_____
_____
_____

• PEW _____

_____
_____
_____
_____
_____
_____
_____
_____
_____
_____

CEREMONY READING SELECTIONS

Source	Selection	Read By	When

BRIDE'S VOWS:

_____

_____

_____

_____

_____

_____

GROOM'S VOWS:

_____

_____

_____

_____

_____

_____

PERSONALIZED RING CEREMONY:

_____

_____

_____

_____

_____

NOTES

UNIQUE
WEDDING IDEAS

IDEAS TO PERSONALIZE YOUR CEREMONY

Regardless of your religious affiliation, there are numerous ways in which you can personalize your wedding ceremony to add a more creative touch. If you're planning a religious ceremony at a church or temple, be sure to discuss all ideas with your officiant.

The following list includes creative ideas to personalize your wedding ceremony:

- Invite the bride's mother to be part of the processional. Have her walk down the aisle with you and your father. (This is the traditional Jewish processional.)

- Invite the groom's parents to be part of the processional as well.

- Ask friends and family members to perform special readings.

- Ask a friend or family member with musical talent to perform at the ceremony.

- Incorporate poetry and/or literature into your readings.

- Change places with the officiant and face your guests during the ceremony.

- Light a unity candle to symbolize your two lives joining together as one.

- Drink wine from a shared "loving" cup to symbolize bonding with each other.

- Hand a rose to each of your mothers as you pass by them during the recessional.

- Release white doves into the air after being pronounced "husband and wife."

- If the ceremony is held outside on a grassy area, have your guests toss flower or grass seeds over you instead of rice.

- Publicly express gratitude for all that your parents have done for you.

- Use a canopy to designate an altar for a non-church setting. Decorate it in ways that are symbolic or meaningful to you.

- Burn incense to give the ceremony an exotic feeling.

IDEAS TO PERSONALIZE YOUR MARRIAGE VOWS

Regardless of your religious affiliation or whether you're planning a church or an outdoor ceremony, there are many ways to personalize your marriage vows in order to make them more meaningful for you. As with all your ceremony plans, be sure to discuss your ideas for marriage vows with your officiant.

The following are some ideas that you might want to consider when planning your marriage vows:

- Discuss with your fiancé if you'd like to write your own personal marriage vows and keep them secret from one another until the actual ceremony.

- Incorporate your guests and family members into your vows by acknowledging their presence at the ceremony.

- Describe what you cherish most about your partner, and what you hope for in your future together.

- Describe your commitment to and love for one another.

- Discuss your feelings and beliefs about marriage.

- If either of you has children from a previous marriage, mention these children in your vows, and discuss your mutual love for and commitment to them.

ATTIRE & BEAUTY

CHOOSING A BRIDAL GOWN IS ONE OF THE MOST IMPORTANT PARTS of planning your wedding. Order your gown six months or more before your wedding as it will need to be made and fitted. Flip through bridal magazines to compare the various styles and shapes and see what appeals to you. If you see a designer you like, call boutiques in your area to see if they carry that line. Have fun trying on dresses!

BRIDAL GOWN

Options: Different gown styles complement different body types. The following are tips to keep in mind when choosing your dress:

A short, heavy figure: To look taller and slimmer, avoid knit fabrics. Use the princess or A-line styles; they flatter any shape. Chiffon is the best fabric choice because it produces a floating effect and camouflages weight.

A short, thin figure: A shirtwaist or natural waist style with bouffant skirt will produce a taller, more rounded figure. Chiffon, velvet, lace, and Schiffli net are the best fabric choices.

A tall, heavy figure: Princess or A-line styles are best for slimming the figure. Satin, chiffon, and lace fabrics are also recommended.

A tall, thin figure: Tiers or flounces will help reduce the impression of height. A shirtwaist or natural waist style with a full skirt are ideal choices. Satin and lace are the best fabrics.

The guidelines below will help you select the most appropriate gown for your wedding:

Informal wedding:
• Street-length gown or suit
• Corsage or small bouquet
• No veil or train

Semiformal wedding:
• Floor-length gown
• Chapel train
• Fingertip veil
• Small bouquet

Formal daytime wedding:
• Floor-length gown
• Chapel or sweep train

- Fingertip veil or hat
- Gloves
- Medium-sized bouquet

Formal evening wedding:
- Same as formal daytime except longer veil

Very formal wedding:
- Floor-length gown
- Cathedral train
- Full-length veil
- Elaborate headpiece
- Long sleeves or long arm-covering gloves
- Cascading bouquet

Things to Consider: When trying on wedding gowns at bridal boutiques, try a variety of styles—you never know what will look amazing on you. Bring your mother, maid of honor, or another close female to have additional opinions. Also, be sure to wear the proper undergarments and a shoe with the heel height you expect to wear on your wedding day.

When ordering a wedding gown, get in writing when your gown will arrive. The gown should arrive at least six weeks before the wedding so you can have it altered and can select the appropriate accessories—jewelry, shoes, gloves, veil, etc. You should have several fittings before your big day to ensure the fit is flawless.

Beware: Some gown manufacturers suggest ordering a size larger than needed. This requires more alterations and extra charges. It is smart to locate a few tailors in your area and ask for alteration pricing in advance. Many boutiques offer tailoring services, but you will often find a better price by finding an independent tailor specializing in bridal gown alterations. Be sure to order your gown with enough time to allow for delivery delays. In addition, it is always smart to check the reputation of the boutique before buying.

Tips to Save Money: Consider renting a gown or buying one secondhand. Renting a gown usually costs about 40 to 60 percent of its retail price. Consider this practical option if you are not planning to preserve the gown. The disadvantage of renting, however, is that your options are more limited, and you can't have it altered for a perfect fit.

Also, ask about discontinued styles and gowns. Watch for clearances and sales, or buy your gown "off the rack." Restore or refurbish a family heirloom gown. If you have a friend, sister, or another family member who is planning a wedding, consider purchasing a gown that you could both wear. Change the veil and headpiece to personalize it.

Price Range: $500 - $10,000

ALTERATIONS

Alterations may be necessary to make your gown fit perfectly and conform smoothly to your body.

Things to Consider: Alterations usually require several fittings. Allow four to six weeks for alterations to be completed. Alterations are usually not included in the cost of the gown.

You may also want to consider making some modifications to your gown, such as shortening or lengthening the train, as well as customizing the sleeves, beading, and so forth. Ask your bridal boutique what they charge for the modifications you desire.

Tips to Save Money: Consider hiring an independent tailor. Their fees are usually lower than those charged at bridal boutiques.

Price Range: $75 - $500

HEADPIECE/VEIL

The headpiece is the part of the bride's outfit to which the veil is attached.

Options for Headpieces: Bow, Garden Hat, Headband, Juliet Cap, Mantilla, Pillbox, Pouf, Tiara

Options for Veils: Ballet, Bird Cage, Blusher, Cathedral Length, Chapel Length, Fingertip, Flyaway

Things to Consider: The headpiece should complement but not overshadow your gown. In addition to the headpiece, you might want a veil. Veils come in different styles and lengths.

Select a length which complements the length of your train. Consider the total look you're trying to achieve with your gown, headpiece, veil, and hairstyle. If possible, schedule your hair "test appointment" the day you go veil shopping—that way, you'll be able to see how your veil looks with your hairstyle.

Tips to Save Money: Some boutiques offer a free headpiece or veil with the purchase of a gown. Make sure you ask about this before purchasing your gown.

Price Range: $60 - $500

GLOVES

Gloves add a nice touch to either short-sleeved, three-quarter length, or sleeveless gowns.

ATTIRE & BEAUTY

Options: Gloves come in various styles and lengths. Depending on the length of your sleeves, select gloves that reach above your elbow, just below your elbow, halfway between your wrist and elbow, or only to your wrist.

Things to Consider: You should not wear gloves if your gown has long sleeves, or if you're planning a small, informal wedding.

Price Range: $15 - $100

JEWELRY

Jewelry can beautifully accent your dress and become the perfect finishing touch.

Options: Consider selecting pieces of jewelry that can be classified as "something old, something new, something borrowed, or something blue" for a festive way to better personalize your look.

Things to Consider: Brides look best with just a few pieces of jewelry — perhaps a string of pearls and earrings. Purchase complementary jewelry for your bridesmaids that match the colors of their dresses. This will give your bridal party a coordinated look.

Price Range: $60 - $2,000

GARTER

It is customary for the bride to wear a garter just above the knee on her wedding day. After the bouquet tossing ceremony, the groom takes the garter off the bride's leg. After all the single men gather on the dance floor, the groom tosses the garter to them over his back. According to age-old tradition, whoever catches the garter is the next to be married!

Things to Consider: You will need to choose the proper music for this event. A popular and fun song to play during the garter removal ceremony is "The Stripper" by David Rose.

Price Range: $15 - $60

SHOES

Options: Wedges, heels, pumps, ballet flats, sandals.

Things to Consider: Make sure you buy beautiful shoes that complement your gown and the formality of your event. For instance, you might wear more casual sandals for a beach wedding or fancy stilettos for a formal affair. Wedges or flat shoes are best for an outdoor wedding, to ensure you don't sink into the ground!

And don't forget to break in your shoes well before your wedding day. Tight shoes can make you miserable on your otherwise perfect day.

Price Range: $50 - $500

BRIDAL HAIR

Many brides prefer to have their hair professionally arranged with their headpiece the day of the wedding rather than try to do it themselves.

Things to Consider: Have your professional hairdresser experiment with your hair and headpiece before your wedding day so there are no surprises. Most hairdressers will include the cost of a sample session in your package. They will try several styles on you and write down the specifics of each one so that everything goes quickly and smoothly on your wedding day. On the big day, you can go to the salon or have the stylist meet you at your home or dressing site. Consider having him or her arrange your bridal party's hair for a consistent look.

Tips to Save Money: Negotiate having your hair arranged free of charge or at a discount in exchange for bringing your mother, your fiancé's mother, and your bridal party to the salon.

Price Range: $50 - $200 per person

MAKEUP ARTIST

A professional makeup artist will apply makeup that should last throughout the day, and will often provide you with samples for touch-ups.

Things to Consider: It's smart to go for a trial run before the day of the wedding so there are no surprises. You can either go to the salon or have the makeup artist meet you at your home or dressing site. Consider having him or her apply makeup for your mother, your fiancé's mother, and your bridesmaids for a consistent look. In selecting a makeup artist, make sure he or she has been trained in makeup for photography. It is very important to wear the proper amount of makeup that will accentuate your features under bright lights and camera flashes, and eliminate any shine on your face.

Consider having your makeup trial right before your hairdresser trial—that way you'll see how your hair looks with your makeup on. It can make a big difference.

Tips to Save Money: Similar to the hair arrangements, try to negotiate having your makeup applied free of charge or at a discount in exchange for bringing your mother, your fiancé's mother, and your wedding party to the salon.

Price Range: $30 - $150 per person

MANICURE/PEDICURE

As a final touch, it's nice to have a professional manicure and/or pedicure the day of your wedding.

Things to Consider: Don't forget to bring the appropriate color nail polish with you for your appointment. You can either go to the salon or have the manicurist meet you at your home or dressing site. Consider having him or her give your mother, your fiancé's mother, and your bridesmaids a manicure in the same color.

Tips to Save Money: Try to negotiate getting a manicure or pedicure free of charge or at a discount in exchange for bringing your mother, your fiancé's mother, and your wedding party to the salon.

Price Range: $15 - $75 per person

GROOM'S FORMAL WEAR

The groom should select his formal wear based on the formality of the wedding. For a semiformal or formal wedding, the groom will need a tuxedo. A tuxedo is the formal jacket worn by men on special or formal occasions. The most popular colors are black, white, and gray.

Options: Use the following guidelines to select customary attire for the groom:

Informal wedding:
- Business suit
- White dress shirt and tie

Semiformal daytime:
- Formal suit
- White dress shirt
- Cummerbund or vest
- Four-in-hand or bow tie

Semiformal evening:
- Formal suit or dinner jacket
- Matching trousers
- White shirt
- Cummerbund or vest
- Black bow tie
- Cuff links and studs

Formal daytime:
- Cutaway or stroller jacket
- Waistcoat
- Striped trousers
- White wing-collared shirt
- Striped tie
- Studs and cuff links

Formal evening:
- Black dinner jacket
- Matching trousers
- Waistcoat
- White tuxedo shirt
- Bow tie
- Cummerbund or vest
- Cuff links

Very formal daytime:
- Cutaway coat
- Wing-collared shirt
- Ascot
- Striped trousers
- Cuff links
- Gloves

Very formal evening:
- Black tailcoat
- Matching striped trousers
- Bow tie
- White wing-collared shirt
- Waistcoat
- Patent leather shoes
- Studs and cuff links
- Gloves

Things to Consider: Reserve tuxedos for yourself and your ushers several weeks before the wedding to ensure a wide selection, and to allow enough time for alterations. Plan to pick up the tuxedos a few days before the wedding so there is time for last-minute adjustments. Ask about the store's return policy and be sure you delegate to the appropriate person (usually your best man) the responsibility of returning all tuxedos within the time allotted. Ushers customarily pay for their own tuxedos. Out-of-town men in your wedding party can be sized at any tuxedo shop and send their measurements directly to the rental store.

Tips to Save Money: Try to negotiate getting your tuxedo for free or at a discount in exchange for having your father, your fiancé's father, and ushers rent their tuxedos at that shop.

Price Range: $60 - $200

BRIDAL ATTIRE CHECKLIST

ITEM	Description	Source
Full Slip		
Garter		
Gloves		
Gown		
Handbag		
Jewelry		
Lingerie		
Panty Hose		
Petticoat or Slip		
Shoes		
Something Old		
Something New		
Something Borrowed		
Something Blue		
Stockings		
Veil/Hat		
Other:		
Other:		
Other:		
Other:		

BRIDAL ATTIRE INFORMATION SHEET

BRIDAL ATTIRE

Bridal Boutique:

Date Ordered:

Salesperson: Phone Number:

Address:

City: State: Zip Code:

Website:

Email:

Description of Dress:

	Manufacturer	Style	Size	Cost
Wedding Gown				
Headpiece				
Veil/Hat				
Shoes				

GOWN ALTERATIONS

Location:

Cost:

Tailor: Phone Number:

Address:

City: State: Zip Code:

Website:

Email:

	Alteration	Date/Time
First Alteration		
Second Alteration		
Third Alteration		
Final Alteration		

BRIDAL BOUTIQUE COMPARISON CHART

QUESTIONS	POSSIBILITY 1	POSSIBILITY 2
What is the name of the bridal boutique?		
What is the website and email of the bridal boutique?		
What is the address of the bridal boutique?		
What is the name and phone number of my contact person?		
What are your hours of operation? Are appointments needed?		
Do you offer any discounts or giveaways?		
What major bridal gown lines do you carry?		
Do you carry outfits for the mother of the bride?		
Do you carry bridesmaids gowns and/or tuxedos?		
Do you carry outfits for the flower girl and ring bearer?		
What is the cost of the desired bridal gown?		
What is the cost of the desired headpiece?		
Do you offer in-house alterations? If so, what are your fees?		
Do you carry bridal shoes? What is the price range?		
Do you dye shoes to match outfits?		
Do you rent bridal slips? If so, what is the rental fee?		
What is the estimated date of delivery for my gown?		
What are your payment and cancellation policies?		

POSSIBILITY 3	POSSIBILITY 4	POSSIBILITY 5	POSSIBILITY 6

BRIDESMAIDS' ATTIRE INFORMATION

Make as many copies of this form as needed.

BRIDESMAIDS' ATTIRE

Bridal Boutique: _____

Date Ordered: _____

Salesperson: _____ Phone Number: _____

Address: _____

City: _____ State: _____ Zip Code: _____

Website: _____

Email: _____

Description of Dress: _____

Cost: _____

Manufacturer: _____

Date Ready: _____

BRIDESMAIDS' SIZES

Name	Dress	Head	Weight	Height	Waist	Gloves	Shoes	Hose

GROOM/USHERS' ATTIRE INFORMATION

Make as many copies of this form as needed.

GROOM/USHERS' ATTIRE

Store Name:

Date Ordered:

Salesperson: Phone Number:

Address:

City: State: Zip Code:

Website:

Email:

Description of Tuxedo:

Cost:

Manufacturer:

Date Ready:

GROOM/USHERS' SIZES

Name	Height	Weight	Waist	Sleeve	Inseam	Jacket	Neck	Shoes

BRIDAL BEAUTY INFORMATION SHEET

APPOINTMENT	Date	Time	Location	Notes
Hair Trial Run				
Makeup Trial Run				
Wedding Day Hair				
Wedding Day Makeup				
Bridesmaids' Hair				
Bridesmaids' Makeup				
Nail Salon				
Other:				
Other:				
Other:				

PHOTOGRAPHY & VIDEOGRAPHY

Karen French

KAREN FRENCH

KAREN FRENCH

KAREN FRENCH

KAREN FRENCH

KAREN FRENCH

PHOTOGRAPHY

THE PHOTOGRAPHS TAKEN AT YOUR WEDDING are the best way to preserve your special day. Chances are you and your fiancé will look at the photos many times during your lifetime. Therefore, hiring a good photographer is one of the most important tasks in planning your wedding.

BRIDE & GROOM'S ALBUM

The bride and groom's photo album is the traditional way of arranging the photographs taken during your special day. Some couples choose to chronicle everything from the proposal to the honeymoon in the album. Others simply use photos from the wedding day. Whichever route you choose, your album will become a treasured keepsake, helping you relive every moment.

Options: Photographers will often put your album together for you as part of a wedding package. There are many different types of wedding albums. They vary in size, color, material, construction, and price. Traditional albums frame each individual photo in a mat on the page. Digitally designed "Montage" albums group the photos in a creatively designed fashion for a more modern look.

Find one that you like and will feel proud to show to your friends and family. Some of the most popular manufacturers are Professional Albums, Leather Craftsman, Capri, and Renaissance.

Keep in mind, however, that the quality of the original photographs will determine how the finished album looks, so choose your photographer for their skills, not necessarily the manufacturer of the album. Make sure you see the different album variations available.

Paper for printing your photos also come in a myriad of options differing in glossiness and texture. Ask to look at samples.

Things to Consider: Make sure you hire a photographer who specializes in weddings. Your photographer should be experienced in wedding procedures, and be familiar with your ceremony and reception sites. This will allow him or her to anticipate your next move, and be in the right place at the right time to capture every special moment. Personal rapport is extremely important. The photographer may be an expert, but if you don't feel comfortable or at ease with him or her, your photography will reflect this. Comfort and compatibility with your photographer can make or break your wedding day and your photographs!

PHOTOGRAPHY

Before hiring a photographer, look at his or her previous work. See if the photographer captured the excitement and emotion of the festivities. Also, remember that the wedding album should unfold like a story book—the story of your wedding. Be sure to discuss the specific moments you want captured with the photographer so that there are no misunderstandings. A good wedding photographer will plan the day with you to ensure you get exactly what you are looking for. It is acceptable to take a list of important photos to your planning session before the wedding.

Be sure to look at the recent photographs on all the potential photographers' websites or blogs. Study the photographers' styles. It's fine if they tell you that they're skilled in "photo journalistic" or "candid" photography, but if that's so, you should see plenty of candid-style shots in their portfolio! Some photographers are known for formal poses, while others specialize in more candid, creative shots. Others can do both. Tell the photographer you choose which style you prefer.

When researching prices, compare the quantity and size of the photographs in your album, as well as the type of album that each photographer will use. Ask how many photos will be taken on average at a wedding of your size. Research and compare the various packages so you can select one that fits your needs.

It is also customary to ask potential photographers for references. Ask to speak to their last three clients, and note the dates of these previous weddings. If the photographers cannot provide references, or if the weddings are dated back several years, choose a different photographer. This means they either don't have very much recent experience photographing weddings, or their most recent clients were not happy with their services.

Beware: Make sure the photographer you interview is the one who will photograph your wedding. Some companies use the work of their best photographer to sell a package, but then send a less-experienced person to the wedding. Your chosen photographer's name should go on your contract.

Also, some churches do not allow photographs to be shot during the ceremony. Enquire about the rules and present them to your photographer so he is knowledgeable about your site.

Tips to Save Money: Consider hiring a professional photographer for the formal shots of your ceremony only. Then ask your guests to take candid shots with their personal cameras and upload them to an online photo website you create. This will save you a considerable amount of money in photography.

To really save money, select a photographer who charges a flat fee to shoot the wedding, and allows you to purchase the digital files immediately afterward. That way, you can print as many photos as you desire for a fraction of the cost.

Price Range: $900 - $9,000

DIY WEDDING ALBUMS

You can also lower the price of your album by paying for the digital files and/or photographs, and then putting them into an album yourself. This is a very time-consuming task, so your photographer may reduce the price of his or her package if you opt to do this.

If you decide to go this route, peruse websites like Shutterfly.com, Blurb.com, or Snapfish.com, which let you design albums using wedding-themed templates. There, you can edit photos, adjust sizes, and even add captions. Or, use photo book software on your computer's hard drive, such as iPhoto for Mac users. With iPhoto, you can create an album using photos directly from your iPhoto gallery, and purchase the finished product from Apple. While PCs don't have an exact equivalent for iPhoto, users can download a plug-in called "Inkubook Photo Book Uploader," that works with Live Photo Gallery for Windows and lets you use photos from your Windows gallery. After you've created your wedding book on your computer, upload it to Inkubook.com, customize it, and order the completed version from the Inkubook website.

Things to Consider: Remember, unless you are a graphic designer, your album probably won't turn out as polished as it would if a professional wedding photographer had created it. You'll be saving money, but you'll also be spending a significant amount of time and energy making it yourself.

That being said, DIY wedding albums make wonderful personalized gifts for guests. Since they are relatively inexpensive, you can create a few and customize the size, format, photos, and captions of each one. Just remember to factor in the cost of additional pages and shipping of each book.

Price Range: $30 - $150

ENGAGEMENT PHOTOS

Many couples are interested in a set of engagement photos to accompany their wedding day photography. These make a nice keepsake for the couple, as well as a gift for friends and family. Many couples decide to use their engagement photos on their Save the Date cards.

Things to Consider: Decide whether you want candid shots, posed portrait shots, or a combination of both. Most couples prefer to have engagement photos taken outside and not in a studio. Ask your photographer if he or she can scout locations. Engagement shoots can include more than one wardrobe change, so bring multiple outfits. Wear bright colors, but refrain from choosing clothing with busy patterns, as they do not photograph as nicely. Also, ask your photographer to take some classic bridal portraits (shots of just the bride).

Tips to Save Money: Consider hiring the same photographer for both your engagement photos and your wedding—many will build the price into the total photography package.

Price Range: $100 - $500

PARENTS' ALBUM

The parents' album is a smaller version of the bride and groom's album. It usually contains about twenty 5" x 7" photographs. Photos should be carefully selected for each individual family. If given as a gift, the album can be personalized with the bride and groom's names, along with the date of their wedding on the front cover. Small "coffee table" books can also be created from digital files that are montaged onto the pages. Ask to see samples of different types of parent albums available.

Tips to Save Money: Try to negotiate at least one free parents' album with the purchase of the bride and groom's album.

Price Range: $100 - $600

PROOFS/PREVIEWS

Photographers will often display a preliminary batch of images on their websites, or provide you with proof DVDs or CDs. That way, you and your spouse can select photographs for your album and for your parents' albums. These photos often contain a watermark so that they cannot be used before payment. A DVD or CD allows you to view your photos in a larger size and more detail.

Things to Consider: When selecting a package, ask how many photos the photographer will take. The more images, the wider the selection you will have to choose from. For a wide selection, the photographer must take at least three to five times the number of prints that will go into your albums.

Ask the photographer how soon after the wedding your proofs or digital files will be available. Request this in writing. Ideally, they will be ready by the time you get back from your honeymoon.

DIGITAL FILES

As previously mentioned, most photographers offer options for purchasing the digital photo files. These files are created as "jpegs," the file type that most labs use to make prints. Your photographer will probably shoot with a professional digital camera that can create extra-large file sizes, which is important for clarity if you want very large prints made (such as 24" x 30" and larger).

Things to Consider: Most photographers today will sell you the rights to the images along with the digital files, so that you can make your own prints. However, many photographers will not provide the digital files up front, since they hope to make a profit from selling prints after the wedding. They, therefore, put the image proofs on their website so that you and your guests purchase the photographs directly from their site.

During your interviews, be sure to ask the photographers how long they keep the files, as well as at what point they will become available to you. A professional photographer should keep a backup copy of the digital files for at least ten years. Some photographers will sell you the entire set of digital files after all photos have been ordered by family and friends. Often the price will vary, depending on the amount spent on re-orders. Once you own your digital files, make a backup copy of your disk every five or six years, as CDs and DVDs can deteriorate after eight years or so.

In addition, there are still some photographers that will not sell the digital files at all. Instead, they simply supply you with a finished album after the wedding. Doing this may reduce the cost of your package, but will also reduce your selection of photographs. In addition, it will most likely be more expensive in the end if you desire additional prints.

Tips to Save Money: If you can wait, consider contacting the photographer a few years later, and ask if he or she will sell you the files at that time. Some photographers will be glad to sell them later at a bargain price.

Price Range: $100 - $800

EXTRA PRINTS

If you are not able to purchase the digital files, you will probably want to purchase extra prints. Extra prints are photographs ordered in addition to the main album or parents' albums. These are usually purchased as gifts for the bridal party, close friends, and family members.

Things to Consider: It is important to discuss the cost of extra prints with your photographer since prices vary considerably. Knowing what extra prints will cost ahead of time will help you know if the photographer is truly within your budget. Think about how many extra prints you would like to order and figure this into your budget before selecting a photographer.

Tips to Save Money: If you can wait, consider not ordering any reprints during the first few years after the wedding to reduce the prices. Some photographers offer them at a bargain price later. You can purchase reprints at this time for a much lower cost.

Price Range: (5" x 7") = $5.00 - $20; (8" x 10") = $15 - $30; (11" x 14") = $30 - $100

PHOTOGRAPHER COMPARISON CHART

QUESTIONS	POSSIBILITY 1	POSSIBILITY 2
What is the name and phone number of the photographer?		
What is the website and email of the photographer?		
What is the address of the photographer?		
How many years of experience do you have as a photographer?		
What percentage of your business is dedicated to weddings?		
Approximately how many weddings have you photographed?		
Are you the person who will photograph my wedding?		
Will you bring an assistant with you to my wedding?		
How do you typically dress for weddings?		
Do you have a professional studio?		
What type of equipment do you use?		
Do you bring backup equipment with you to weddings?		
Do you need to visit the ceremony and reception sites prior to the wedding?		
Do you have liability insurance?		
Are you skilled in diffused lighting and soft focus?		
Can you take studio portraits?		
Can you retouch my images?		

POSSIBILITY 3	POSSIBILITY 4	POSSIBILITY 5	POSSIBILITY 6

PHOTOGRAPHER COMPARISON CHART (CONT'D)

QUESTIONS	POSSIBILITY 1	POSSIBILITY 2
Can digital files be purchased? If so, when, and what is the cost?		
What is the cost of the package I am interested in?		
What is your payment policy?		
What is your cancellation policy?		
Do you offer a money-back guarantee?		
Do you use paper proofs or digital proofing?		
How many photographs will I have to choose from?		
When will I get my proofs?		
When will I get my album?		
What is the cost of an engagement portrait?		
What is the cost of a formal bridal portrait?		
What is the cost of a parent album?		
What is the cost of a 5 x 7 reprint?		
What is the cost of an 8 x 10 reprint?		
What is the cost of an 11 x 14 reprint?		
What is the cost per additional hour of shooting at the wedding?		

PHOTOGRAPHER COMPARISON CHART (CONT'D)

POSSIBILITY 3	POSSIBILITY 4	POSSIBILITY 5	POSSIBILITY 6

PHOTOGRAPHER'S INFORMATION

Once it is completed, make a copy of this form to give to your photographer as a reminder of your various events.

THE WEDDING OF: Phone Number:

PHOTOGRAPHER'S COMPANY

Business Name:

Address:

City: State: Zip Code:

Website: Email:

Photographer's Name: Phone Number:

Assistant's Name: Phone Number:

ENGAGEMENT PHOTOS

Date: Time:

Location:

Address:

City: State: Zip Code:

BRIDAL PORTRAIT

Date: Time:

Location:

Address:

City: State: Zip Code:

PHOTOGRAPHER'S INFORMATION

Once it is completed, make a copy of this form to give to your
photographer as a reminder of your various events.

OTHER EVENTS

Event:

Date: _____ Time:

Location:

Address:

City: _____ State: _____ Zip Code:

CEREMONY

Date: _____ Arrival Time: _____ Departure Time:

Location:

Address:

City: _____ State: _____ Zip Code:

Ceremony Restrictions/Guidelines:

RECEPTION

Date: _____ Arrival Time: _____ Departure Time:

Location:

Address:

City: _____ State: _____ Zip Code:

Reception Restrictions/Guidelines:

WEDDING PHOTOGRAPHS

Check off all photographs you would like taken throughout your wedding day.
Then make a copy of this form and give it to your photographer.

PRE-CEREMONY PHOTOGRAPHS

- ❑ Bride leaving her house
- ❑ Wedding rings with the invitation
- ❑ Bride getting dressed for the ceremony
- ❑ Bride looking at her bouquet
- ❑ Maid of honor putting garter on bride's leg
- ❑ Bride alone
- ❑ Bride with her mother
- ❑ Bride with her father
- ❑ Bride with mother and father
- ❑ Bride with her entire family and/or any combination thereof
- ❑ Bride with her maid of honor
- ❑ Bride with her bridesmaids
- ❑ Bride with the flower girl and/or ring bearer
- ❑ Bride's mother putting on her corsage
- ❑ Groom leaving his house
- ❑ Groom putting on his boutonniere
- ❑ Groom with his mother
- ❑ Groom with his father
- ❑ Groom with mother and father
- ❑ Groom with his entire family and/or any combination thereof
- ❑ Groom with his best man
- ❑ Groom with his ushers
- ❑ Groom shaking hands with his best man
- ❑ Groom with the bride's father
- ❑ Bride and her father getting out of the limousine
- ❑ Special members of the family being seated
- ❑ Groom waiting for the bride before the processional
- ❑ Bride and her father just before the processional

WEDDING PHOTOGRAPHS

Check off all photographs you would like taken throughout your wedding day.
Then make a copy of this form and give it to your photographer.

OTHER PRE-CEREMONY PHOTOGRAPHS YOU WOULD LIKE

❑ _____
❑ _____
❑ _____
❑ _____
❑ _____

CEREMONY PHOTOGRAPHS

❑ The processional
❑ Bride and groom saying their vows
❑ Bride and groom exchanging rings
❑ Groom kissing the bride at the altar
❑ The recessional

OTHER CEREMONY PHOTOS YOU WOULD LIKE

❑ _____
❑ _____
❑ _____
❑ _____
❑ _____

POST-CEREMONY PHOTOGRAPHS

❑ Bride and groom
❑ Newlyweds with both of their families
❑ Newlyweds with the entire wedding party
❑ Bride and groom signing the marriage certificate
❑ Flowers and other decorations

OTHER POST-CEREMONY PHOTOS YOU WOULD LIKE

❑ _____
❑ _____
❑ _____
❑ _____
❑ _____

WEDDING PHOTOGRAPHS

Check off all photographs you would like taken throughout your wedding day.
Then make a copy of this form and give it to your photographer.

RECEPTION PHOTOGRAPHS

❑ Entrance of newlyweds and wedding party into the reception site
❑ Receiving line
❑ Guests signing the guest book
❑ Toasts
❑ First dance
❑ Bride and her father dancing
❑ Groom and his mother dancing
❑ Bride dancing with groom's father
❑ Groom dancing with bride's mother
❑ Wedding party and guests dancing
❑ Cake table
❑ Cake cutting ceremony
❑ Couple feeding each other cake
❑ Table decorations
❑ Bouquet-tossing ceremony
❑ Garter-tossing ceremony
❑ Musicians
❑ The wedding party table
❑ The family tables
❑ Candid shots of your guests
❑ Bride and groom saying goodbye to their parents
❑ Bride and groom looking back, waving goodbye in the getaway car

OTHER RECEPTION PHOTOS YOU WOULD LIKE

❑ _____
❑ _____
❑ _____
❑ _____
❑ _____
❑ _____
❑ _____
❑ _____
❑ _____

VIDEOGRAPHY

NEXT TO YOUR PHOTO ALBUM, VIDEOGRAPHY IS THE best way to preserve your wedding memories. Videography captures the emotions, laughter, and mood of the wedding day in motion and sound, and makes a wonderful gift for anyone who might be unable to attend the event. Wedding videos are edited and professionally produced with music, slow motion, black and white scenes, titles, and many other special features.

Today's wedding videos can be edited and professionally produced. You have the option of selecting one, two, or three cameras to record your wedding. The more cameras used, the more action your videographer can capture—and the more expensive the service. An experienced videographer, however, can do a good job with just one camera.

Options: There are two basic types of wedding video production: documentary and cinematic. The documentary type production records your wedding day as it happened in real time. Very little editing or embellishment is involved. These types of videos are normally less expensive and can be delivered within days after the wedding.

The cinematic type production is more reminiscent of a movie. Although it can be shot with one camera, most cinematic wedding videos are shot with two cameras, allowing one videographer to focus on the events as they happen, while the other gathers footage that will be added later to enhance the final result. This type of video requires more time due to the extensive editing of the footage, which can take up to 40 hours of studio time.

You may wish to have both of these types of videos—one straightforward version and another version focusing on the details with a nice, theatrical flow.

Consider having your ceremony shot in high definition. While HD equipment is more expensive, this is the best way to ensure that you'll be able to enjoy watching your wedding video in a crisp, clear resolution for years to come.

MAIN VIDEO

You will need to choose the type of video you want. Do you want the footage edited down to a 30-minute film, or do you want an "as it happened" replay? Remember, an edited video will require more time, and will therefore be more expensive than just a documentary of the events.

VIDEOGRAPHY

Things to Consider: Be sure to hire a videographer who specializes in weddings and ask to see samples of his or her work. Weddings are very specialized events. A $1,000 video camera in the hands of a seasoned professional "wedding" videographer will produce far better results than a $3,000 broadcast quality camera, or a $4,000 high definition camera in the hands of just an average camera operator. When considering a particular videographer, look at previous weddings the videographer has filmed. Notice the color and brightness of the screen, as well as the quality of sound. This will indicate the quality of his or her equipment. Note whether the picture is smooth or jerky; you will be able to tell the videographer's skill level. Ask about special effects such as titles, dissolve, and multiple screens. Find out what's included in the cost of your package so that there are no surprises at the end!

If you will be getting married in a church, find out the church's policies regarding videography. Some churches might require the videographer to film the ceremony from a specific distance.

Beware: As in photography, there are many companies with more than one videographer. These companies may use the work of their best videographer to sell their packages and then send a less experienced videographer to the wedding. Again, don't get caught in this trap! Be sure to interview the videographer who will shoot your wedding so you can get a good idea of his or her style and personality. Ask to see his or her work.

Tips to Save Money: Compare videographers' quality, value, and price. There is a wide range, and the most expensive is not necessarily the best. The videographer who uses one camera (instead of multiple cameras) is usually the most cost-effective, and may be all you need.

Consider hiring a company that offers both videography and photography. You might save money by combining the two services.

Ask a family member or close friend to film your wedding. However, realize that without professional equipment and expertise, the final product may not be quite as polished.

Price Range: $600 - $4,000

TITLES

Titles and subtitles can be edited into your video before or after the filming. Titles are important, since twenty years from now you might not remember the exact time of your wedding or the names of your bridal party members. Some videographers charge more for titling. Make sure you discuss this with your videographer and get in writing exactly what titles will be included.

Options: Titles can include the date, time, and location of the wedding, the bride and groom's names, as well as the names of special family members and bridal party. Titles may also include special thanks to those who helped with the wedding. You can then send these people copies of your video, which would be a very appropriate and inexpensive gift!

Tips to Save Money: Consider asking for limited titles, such as only the names of the bride and groom, the date, and the time of the wedding.

Price Range: $50 - $300

EXTRA HOURS

Find out how much your videographer would charge to stay longer than the contracted time. Do this in case your reception lasts longer than expected. Don't forget to get this fee in writing.

Tips to Save Money: To avoid paying for hours beyond what's included in your selected package, calculate the maximum number of hours you think you'll need, and negotiate that number of hours into your package price.

To reduce the amount of time you'll need to use the videographer, consider recording the ceremony only.

Price Range: $35 - $150 per hour

PHOTO MONTAGE

You might also ask if your videographer can incorporate old photos or video footage into your wedding video. It can be fun to include baby pictures, childhood video footage, or still images of the two of you in a photo montage, in addition to shots from your rehearsal, wedding day, honeymoon, or any combination thereof.

Things to Consider: Send copies of your photo montage video to close friends and family members as mementos of your wedding.

Tips to Save Money: There are many websites that allow you to create your own photo montage either for free or at a very low price. You can then transfer your photo montage to a DVD.

Price Range: $60 - $300

VIDEOGRAPHY

EXTRA COPIES

Ask your videographer what the charge is for extra copies. Before burning your own copies of your wedding DVD, be sure to ask your videographer if that is acceptable. Many contracts prohibit it, and doing so could be copyright infringement. Further, your videographer may have put a security device on the DVD that would prevent you from being able to copy it.

Price Range: $15 - $50

SAME DAY EDIT

Some videographers also offer something called a Same Day Edit, which is a short, 2 to 6-minute compilation video that the videographer shoots before and during the ceremony, then edits on-site and presents at the reception, recapping the highlights of your day. This is always an unexpected treat for guests that will have everyone laughing and crying.

Things to Consider: You will need to have projection equipment and a screen to show your Same Day Edit video. Check to see if your videographer can provide this equipment, otherwise it will need to be rented.

Price Range: $200 - $1,000

VIDEOGRAPHER'S INFORMATION

Once it is completed, make a copy of this form to give to your videographer as a reminder of your various events.

THE WEDDING OF: Phone Number:

VIDEOGRAPHER'S COMPANY:

Business Name:

Address:

City: State: Zip Code:

Website:

Email:

Videographer's Name: Phone Number:

Assistant's Name: Phone Number:

CEREMONY:

Date: Arrival Time: Departure Time:

Location:

Address:

City: State: Zip Code:

Ceremony Restrictions/Guidelines:

RECEPTION:

Date: Arrival Time: Departure Time:

Location:

Address:

City: State: Zip Code:

Reception Restrictions/Guidelines:

VIDEOGRAPHY COMPARISON CHART

QUESTIONS	POSSIBILITY 1	POSSIBILITY 2
What is the name and phone number of the videographer?		
What is the website and email address of the videographer?		
What is the address of the videographer?		
How many years of experience do you have as a videographer?		
Approximately how many weddings have you filmed?		
Are you the person who will film my wedding?		
Will you bring an assistant with you to my wedding?		
What type of equipment do you use?		
Do you have a wireless microphone?		
Do you bring backup equipment with you?		
Do you visit the ceremony and reception sites before the wedding?		
Do you edit the footage after the event?		
Who keeps the raw footage and for how long?		
When will I receive the final product?		
What is the cost of the desired package?		
What does it include?		
Can you make a photo montage? What is the cost?		
Can you do a Same Day Edit? What is the cost?		
What is your payment policy?		
What is your cancellation policy?		

POSSIBILITY 3	POSSIBILITY 4	POSSIBILITY 5	POSSIBILITY 6

NOTES

STATIONERY
& RECEPTION

Karen French

STATIONERY

BEGIN CREATING YOUR GUEST LIST AS SOON AS POSSIBLE. Ask your parents and the groom's parents for a list of people they would like to invite. You and your fiancé should make your own lists. Make certain that all names are spelled correctly and that all addresses are current. Determine if you wish to include children; if so, add their names to your list. Traditionally, all children over the age of 16 receive their own invitation.

INVITATIONS

Order your invitations at least four months before the wedding. Allow an additional month for engraved invitations. Invitations are traditionally issued by the bride's parents; but if the groom's parents will assume some of the wedding expenses, the invitations should include their names as well. Mail all invitations six to eight weeks before the wedding.

Options: There are three types of invitations: traditional/formal, contemporary, and informal. The traditional/formal wedding invitation is white, soft cream, or ivory with raised black lettering. The printing is done on the top page of a double sheet of thick quality paper; the inside is left blank. The contemporary invitation is typically a personalized presentation that makes a statement.

Informal invitations are often printed on the front of a single, heavyweight card, and may be handwritten or preprinted.

There are many types of printing, but the most popular today include engraved, thermography,

digital, and offset printing. Engraving is the most expensive, traditional, and formal type of printing. It also takes the longest to complete. In engraved printing, stationery is pressed onto a copper plate, which makes the letters rise slightly from the page. Thermography is a process that fuses powder and ink to create a raised letter. This takes less time than engraving, and is less expensive because the copper plates do not have to be engraved. Offset printing is a common practice in which the inked image is burned onto a plate and then applied to the printing surface. It works on a plethora of materials such as wood, cloth, metal, and leather. Finally, digital printing is the cheapest, quickest, and least formal option.

Things to Consider: If all your guests are to be invited to both the ceremony and the reception, a combined invitation may be sent without separate enclosure cards. Order one invitation for each married or cohabiting couple that you plan to invite. The officiant and his or her spouse, as well as your attendants, should also receive an invitation.

Order approximately 20 percent more stationery than your actual count, just in case. Allow a minimum of two weeks to address and mail the invitations, longer if using a calligrapher or if your guest list is very large. You may also want to consider ordering invitations for the rehearsal dinner, as these should be in the same style as the wedding invitation.

SAMPLES OF TRADITIONAL/FORMAL INVITATIONS

1) When the bride's parents sponsor the wedding:

Mr. and Mrs. Alexander Waterman Smith
request the honor of your presence
at the marriage of their daughter,
Miss Carol Ann
to
Mr. William James Clark
on Saturday, the fifth of August
two thousand and twelve
at two o'clock in the afternoon
Saint James by-the-Sea
La Jolla, California

2) When the groom's parents sponsor the wedding:

Mr. and Mrs. Michael Burdell Clark
request the honor of your presence
at the marriage of
Miss Carol Ann Smith
to their son,
Mr. William James Clark

3) When both the bride and groom's parents sponsor the wedding:

Mr. and Mrs. Alexander Waterman Smith
and
Mr. and Mrs. Michael Burdell Clark
request the honor of your presence
at the marriage of their children,
Miss Carol Ann Smith
to
Mr. William James Clark

OR

Mr. and Mrs. Alexander Waterman Smith
request the honor of your presence
at the marriage of their daughter,
Miss Carol Ann Smith
to
William James Clark,
son of Mr. and Mrs. Michael Burdell Clark

4) When the bride and groom sponsor their own wedding:

The honor of your presence is requested
at the marriage of
Miss Carol Ann Smith
and
Mr. William James Clark

OR

Miss Carol Ann Smith
and
Mr. William James Clark
request the honor of your presence
at their marriage

5) With divorced or deceased parents:

a) When the bride's mother is sponsoring the wedding and is not remarried:

Mrs. Julie Hurden Smith
requests the honor of your presence
at the marriage of her daughter,
Miss Carol Ann

b) When the bride's mother is sponsoring the wedding and has remarried:

Mrs. Julie Hurden Booker
requests the honor of your presence
at the marriage of her daughter,
Miss Carol Ann Smith

OR

Mr. and Mrs. John Thomas Booker
request the honor of your presence
at the marriage of Mrs. Booker's daughter,
Miss Carol Ann Smith

c) When the bride's father is sponsoring the wedding and has not remarried:

Mr. Alexander Waterman Smith
requests the honor of your presence
at the marriage of his daughter,
Miss Carol Ann

d) When the bride's father is sponsoring the wedding and has remarried:

Mr. and Mrs. Alexander Waterman Smith
request the honor of your presence
at the marriage of Mr. Smith's daughter,
Miss Carol Ann

6) **With deceased parents:**

a) When a close friend or relative sponsors the wedding:

Mr. and Mrs. Brandt Elliott Lawson
request the honor of your presence
at the marriage of their granddaughter,
Miss Carol Ann Smith

7) **In military ceremonies, the rank determines the placement of names:**

a) Any title lower than sergeant should be omitted. Only the branch of service should be included under that person's name:

Mr. and Mrs. Alexander Waterman Smith
request the honor of your presence
at the marriage of their daughter,
Miss Carol Ann
to
William James Clark
United States Army

b) Junior officers' titles are placed below their names and are followed by their branch of service:

Mr. and Mrs. Alexander Waterman Smith
request the honor of your presence
at the marriage of their daughter,
Miss Carol Ann
to
William James Clark
First Lieutenant, United States Army

c) If the rank is higher than lieutenant, titles are placed before names, and the branch of service is placed on the following line:

Mr. and Mrs. Alexander Waterman Smith
request the honor of your presence
at the marriage of their daughter,
Miss Carol Ann
to
Captain William James Clark
United States Navy

SAMPLE OF A LESS FORMAL/MORE CONTEMPORARY INVITATION

Mr. and Mrs. Alexander Waterman Smith
would like you to
join with their daughter
Carol Ann
and
William James Clark
in the celebration of their marriage

For additional wording suggestions, log on to www.WeddingSolutions.com.

Tips to Save Money: Thermography looks like engraving and is one-third the cost. Choose paper stock that is reasonable, yet achieves your overall look. Select invitations that can be mailed using just one stamp. Order at least 25 extra invitations in case you soil some or add people to your list. To reorder this small number of invitations later would cost nearly three times the amount you'll spend up front.

Price Range: $0.75 - $6 per invitation

RESPONSE CARDS

Response cards are enclosed with the invitation to determine the number of people who will be attending your wedding. They are the smallest card size accepted by the postal service and should be printed in the same style as the invitation. An invitation to only the wedding ceremony does not usually include a request for a reply. However, response cards should be used when it is necessary to have an exact head count for special seating arrangements. Response cards are widely accepted today. If included, these cards should be easy for your guests to understand and use. Include a self-addressed and stamped return envelope to make it easy for your guests to return the response cards.

Things to Consider: You should not include a line that reads "number of persons" on your response cards, because only those whose names appear on the inner and outer envelopes are invited. Each couple, each single person, and all children over the age of 16 should receive their own invitation. Indicate on the inner envelope if they may bring an escort or guest. Omitting children's names from the inner envelope infers that the children are not invited.

Samples of wording for response cards:

M_____

(The M may be eliminated from the line, especially if many doctors are invited)

___ accepts

___ regrets

Saturday the fifth of July

Oceanside Country Club

OR

The favor of your reply is requested

by the twenty-second of May

M_____

will _____ attend

Price Range: $0.40 - $1 each

RECEPTION CARDS

If the guest list for the ceremony is larger than the one for the reception, a separate card with the date, time, and location for the reception should be enclosed with the ceremony invitation for those guests also invited to the reception. Reception cards should be placed in front of the invitation, facing the back flap and the person inserting them. They should be printed on the same quality paper and in the same style as the invitation itself.

Sample of a formally worded reception card:

Mr. and Mrs. Alexander Waterman Smith
request the pleasure of your company
Saturday, the third of July
at three o'clock
Oceanside Country Club
2020 Waterview Lane
Oceanside, California

Sample of a less formal reception card:

Reception immediately following the ceremony
Oceanside Country Club
2020 Waterview Lane
Oceanside, California

Things to Consider: You may also include a reception card in all your invitations if the reception is to be held at a different site than the ceremony.

Tips to Save Money: If all people invited to the ceremony are also invited to the reception, include the reception information on the invitation, and eliminate the reception card. This will save printing and postage costs.

Price Range: $0.40 - $1 each

For additional wording suggestions, log on to www.WeddingSolutions.com.

CEREMONY CARDS

If the guest list for the reception is longer than the one for the ceremony, you should include a special insertion card with the date, time, and location for the ceremony with the reception invitation for those guests also invited to the ceremony,

Place ceremony cards in front of the invitation, facing the back flap and the person inserting them. The cards should be printed on the same quality paper and in the same style as the invitation itself.

Price Range: $0.40 - $1 each

PEW CARDS

Pew cards may be used to let special guests and family members know they are to be seated in the reserved section on either the bride's side or the groom's side. These are most typically seen in large, formal ceremonies. Guests should take this card to the ceremony, and show it to the ushers, who should then escort them to their seats.

Options: Pew cards may indicate a specific pew number if specific seats are assigned, or may read "Within the Ribbon" if certain pews are reserved, but no specific seat is assigned.

Things to Consider: Pew cards may be inserted along with the invitation, or may be sent separately after the RSVPs have been returned. It is often easier to send them after you have received all RSVPs so you know how many reserved pews will be needed.

Tips to Save Money: Include the pew card with the invitation to special guests and simply write, "Within the Ribbon." After you have received all the RSVPs, you will know how many pews need to be reserved. This will save you the cost of mailing the pew cards separately.

Price Range: $0.25 - $1 each

SEATING/PLACE CARDS

Seating/place cards are used to let guests know where they should be seated at the reception, and are a good way of putting people together so they feel most comfortable. Place cards should be laid out alphabetically on a table at the entrance to the reception. Each card should correspond to a table—either by number, color, or another identifying factor. Every table should be marked accordingly.

Options: Select a traditional or contemporary design for your place cards, depending on the style of your wedding.

Regardless of the design, place cards must contain the same information: the bride and groom's names are on the first line; the date is on the second line; the third line is left blank for you to write in the guest's name; and the fourth line is for the table number, color, or another identifying factor.

Price Range: $0.25 - $1 each

RAIN CARDS

These cards are enclosed when guests are invited to an outdoor ceremony and/or reception, informing them of an alternate location in case of bad weather. As with other enclosures, rain cards should be placed in front of the invitation, facing the back flap and the person inserting them. They should be printed on the same quality paper and in the same style as the invitation itself.

Price Range: $0.25 - $1 each

MAPS

Maps to the ceremony and/or reception are becoming frequent inserts in wedding invitations. They should to be drawn and printed in the same style as the invitation, and are usually on a small, heavier card. If they are not printed in the same style or on the same type of paper as the invitation, they should be mailed separately.

Options: Maps should include both written and visual instructions, keeping in mind that guests may be coming from different locations.

Things to Consider: Order extra maps to hand out at the ceremony if the reception is at a different location.

Tips to Save Money: If you are comfortable with computers, you can purchase software that allows you to draw your own maps. Print a map to both the ceremony and reception on the same sheet of paper, perhaps one on each side. This will save you the cost of mailing two maps. Or have your ushers hand out maps to the reception after the ceremony.

Price Range: $0.50 - $1 each

CEREMONY PROGRAMS

Ceremony programs are printed documents showing the sequence of events during the ceremony. These programs add a personal touch to your wedding, and are a convenient way of letting guests know the names of your attendants, officiant, and ceremony musicians.

Options: Ceremony programs can be handed out by the ushers, or they can be placed at the back of the church for guests to take as they enter.

Price Range: $0.75 - $3 each

STATIONERY

ANNOUNCEMENTS

Announcements are not obligatory, but serve a useful purpose. They may be sent to friends who are not invited to the wedding because the number of guests must be limited, or because they live too far away. They may also be sent to acquaintances who, while not particularly close to the family, might still wish to know about the marriage.

Announcements are also appropriate for friends and acquaintances who are not expected to attend, and for whom you do not want to give an obligation of sending a gift. They should include the day, month, year, city, and state where the ceremony took place.

Things to Consider: Announcements should never be sent to anyone who has received an invitation to the ceremony or the reception. They are printed on the same paper and in the same style as the invitation. They should be addressed before the wedding and mailed the day of or the day after the ceremony.

Price Range: $0.75 - $2 each

THANK YOU NOTES

Regardless of whether the couple has thanked the donor in person or not, they must write a thank you note for every gift received.

Things to Consider: Order thank you notes along with your other stationery at least four months before your wedding. You should order some with your maiden initials for thank you notes sent before the ceremony, and the rest with your married initials for notes sent after the wedding, as well as for future use. Send thank you notes within two weeks of receiving a gift that arrives before the wedding, and within two months after the honeymoon for gifts received on or after your wedding day. Be sure to mention the gift you received in the body of the note, and let the person know how much you like it and what you plan to do with it.

Price Range: $0.40 - $0.75 each

STAMPS

Don't forget to budget stamps for response cards as well as for invitations!

Things to Consider: Don't order stamps until you have had the post office weigh your completed invitation. It may exceed the size and weight for one stamp. Order commemorative stamps that fit the occasion.

Price Range: $0.44 - $1 per each invitation

CALLIGRAPHY

Calligraphy is a form of elegant handwriting often used to address invitations for formal occasions. Traditional wedding invitations are addressed in black or blue fountain pen.

Options: You may address the invitations yourself, hire a professional calligrapher, or have your invitations addressed using calligraphy type via a computer. Make sure you use the same method or person to address both the inner and outer envelopes.

Tips to Save Money: You may want to consider taking a short course to learn the art of calligraphy so that you can address your own invitations. If you have a computer with a laser printer, you can address the invitations yourself using one of the many beautiful calligraphy fonts available.

Price Range: $0.50 - $3 each

NAPKINS/MATCHBOOKS

Napkins and matchbooks may also be ordered from your stationer. These are placed around the reception room as decorative items and mementos of the event.

Things to Consider: Napkins and matchbooks can be printed in your wedding colors, or simply white with gold or silver lettering. Include both of your names and the wedding date. You may consider including a phrase or thought, or a small graphic design above your names.

Price Range: $0.50 - $1.50 each

STATIONERY CHECKLIST

STATIONERY ITEM	Quantity	Cost
❏ Invitations		
❏ Envelopes		
❏ Response Cards/Envelopes		
❏ Reception Cards		
❏ Ceremony Cards		
❏ Pew Cards		
❏ Seating/Place Cards		
❏ Rain Cards		
❏ Maps		
❏ Ceremony Programs		
❏ Announcements		
❏ Thank You Notes		
❏ Stamps		
❏ Personalized Napkins/Matchbooks		
❏ Other:		
❏ Other:		
❏ Other:		

Make as many copies of this form as needed.

Name:

Address:

City:

State: Zip Code:

Phone Number:

Email:

Name:

Address:

City:

State: Zip Code:

Phone Number:

Email:

Name:

Address:

City:

State: Zip Code:

Phone Number:

Email:

Name:

Address:

City:

State: Zip Code:

Phone Number:

Email:

Name:

Address:

City:

State: Zip Code:

Phone Number:

Email:

Name:

Address:

City:

State: Zip Code:

Phone Number:

Email:

Name:

Address:

City:

State: Zip Code:

Phone Number:

Email:

Name:

Address:

City:

State: Zip Code:

Phone Number:

Email:

SAMPLE CEREMONY PROGRAM

The Marriage of
Carol Ann Smith and William James Clark
the eleventh of March, 2012
San Diego, California

OUR CEREMONY

Prelude:
"All I Ask of You" by Andrew Lloyd Webber

Processional:
"Canon in D Major" by Pachelbel

Rite of Marriage

Welcome guests

Statement of intentions

Marriage vows

Exchange of rings

Blessing of bride and groom

Pronouncement of marriage

Presentation of the bride and groom

Recessional:
"Trumpet Voluntary" by Jeremiah Clarke

OUR WEDDING PARTY

Maid of Honor:
Susan Smith, Sister of Bride

Best Man:
Brandt Clark, Brother of Groom

Bridesmaids:
Janet Anderson, Friend of Bride
Lisa Bennett, Friend of Bride

Ushers:
Mark Gleason, Friend of Groom
Tommy Olson, Friend of Groom

Officiant:
Father Henry Thomas

OUR RECEPTION

Please join us after the ceremony
in the celebration of our marriage at:
La Valencia Hotel
1132 Prospect Street
La Jolla, California

STATIONERY COMPARISON CHART

QUESTIONS	POSSIBILITY 1	POSSIBILITY 2
What is the name and phone number of the stationery provider?		
What is the website and email of the stationery provider?		
What is the address of the stationery provider?		
How many years of experience do you have?		
What lines of stationery do you carry?		
What types of printing processes do you offer?		
How soon in advance does the order have to be placed?		
What is the turnaround time?		
What is the cost of the desired invitation? Announcement?		
What is the cost of the desired response card? Reception card?		
What is the cost of the desired thank you note?		
What is the cost of the desired party favors?		
What is the cost of the desired wedding program?		
What is the cost of addressing the envelopes in calligraphy?		
What is your payment policy?		
What is your cancellation policy?		

POSSIBILITY 3	POSSIBILITY 4	POSSIBILITY 5	POSSIBILITY 6

STATIONERY DESCRIPTION

STATIONER: _____   Date Ordered: _____

Salesperson: _____   Phone Number: _____

Address: _____

City: _____   State: _____   Zip Code: _____

Website: _____

Email: _____

STATIONERY ITEM: (Include selections for Paper, Style, Color, Font, Printing)

Invitations/Envelopes: _____

Response Cards/Envelopes: _____

Reception Cards: _____

Ceremony Cards: _____

Pew Cards: _____

Seating/Place Cards: _____

Rain Cards: _____

Maps: _____

Ceremony Programs: _____

Announcements: _____

Thank You Notes: _____

Napkins: _____

Matchbooks: _____

Invitations:

_____

_____

_____

_____

_____

_____

Announcements:

_____

_____

Reception Cards:

_____

_____

Response Cards:

_____

_____

Seating/Place Cards:

_____

_____

Napkins/Matchbooks:

_____

_____

GUEST AND GIFT LIST

Make as many copies of this form as needed.

Name:
Address:
City:
State: Zip Code:
Phone Number:
Email:
Table/Pew #:
Shower Gift:
❑ Thank You Note Sent
Wedding Gift:
❑ Thank You Note Sent

Name:
Address:
City:
State: Zip Code:
Phone Number:
Email:
Table/Pew #:
Shower Gift:
❑ Thank You Note Sent
Wedding Gift:
❑ Thank You Note Sent

Name:
Address:
City:
State: Zip Code:
Phone Number:
Email:
Table/Pew #:
Shower Gift:
❑ Thank You Note Sent
Wedding Gift:
❑ Thank You Note Sent

Name:
Address:
City:
State: Zip Code:
Phone Number:
Email:
Table/Pew #:
Shower Gift:
❑ Thank You Note Sent
Wedding Gift:
❑ Thank You Note Sent

Name:
Address:
City:
State: Zip Code:
Phone Number:
Email:
Table/Pew #:
Shower Gift:
❑ Thank You Note Sent
Wedding Gift:
❑ Thank You Note Sent

Name:
Address:
City:
State: Zip Code:
Phone Number:
Email:
Table/Pew #:
Shower Gift:
❑ Thank You Note Sent
Wedding Gift:
❑ Thank You Note Sent

ADDRESSING
INVITATIONS

WE RECOMMEND THAT YOU START ADDRESSING YOUR INVITATIONS at least three months before your wedding, and preferably four months if you are using calligraphy or if your guest list is above 200. You may want to ask your maid of honor or bridesmaids to help you with this time-consuming task, as this is traditionally part of their responsibilities. Organize a luncheon or get-together with hors d'oeuvres and make a party out of it! If you are working with a wedding consultant, he or she can also help you address invitations.

There are typically two envelopes that need to be addressed for wedding invitations: an inner envelope and an outer envelope. The inner envelope is placed unsealed inside the outer envelope, with the flap away from the person inserting.

The invitation and all enclosures are placed inside the inner envelope facing the back flap. The inner envelope contains the name (or names) of the person (or people) who are invited to the ceremony and/or reception. The address is not included on the inner envelope.

The outer envelope contains the name (or names) and address of the person (or people) to whom the inner envelope belongs.

Use the guidelines on the following page to help you properly address both the inner and outer envelopes.

GUIDELINES FOR ADDRESSING INVITATIONS

SITUATION	INNER ENVELOPE No first name or address	OUTER ENVELOPE Has first name & address
Husband and Wife (with same surname)	Mr. and Mrs. Smith	Mr. and Mrs. Thomas Smith (use middle name, if known)
Husband and Wife (with different surnames)	Ms. Banks and Mr. Smith (wife first)	Ms. Anita Banks Mr. Thomas Smith (wife's name & title above husband's)
Husband and Wife (wife has professional title)	Dr. Smith and Mr. Smith	Dr. Anita Smith Mr. Thomas Smith (wife's name & title above husband's)
Husband and Wife (with children under 16)	Mr. and Mrs. Smith John, Mary, and Glen (in order of age)	Mr. and Mrs. Thomas Smith
Single Woman (regardless of age)	Miss/Ms. Smith	Miss/Ms. Beverly Smith
Single Woman and Guest	Miss/Ms. Smith Mr. Jones (or "and Guest")	Miss/Ms. Beverly Smith
Single Man	Mr. Jones (Master for a young boy)	Mr. William Jones
Single Man and Guest	Mr. Jones Miss/Ms. Smith (or "and Guest")	Mr. William Jones
Unmarried Couple Living Together	Mr. Knight and Ms. Orlandi (names listed alphabetically)	Mr. Michael Knight Ms. Paula Orlandi
Two Sisters (over 16)	The Misses Smith	The Misses Mary and Jane Smith (in order of age)
Two Brothers (over 16)	The Messrs. Smith	The Messrs. John and Glen Smith (in order of age)
Brothers & Sisters (over 16)	Mary, Jane, John & Glen (name the girls first, in order of age)	The Misses Smith The Messrs. Smith (name the girls first)
A Brother and Sister (over 16)	Jane and John (name the girl first)	Miss Jane Smith and Mr. John Smith (name the girl first)
Widow	Mrs. Smith	Mrs. William Smith
Divorcée	Mrs. Smith	Mrs. Jones Smith (maiden name and former husband's surname)

RECEPTION

THE RECEPTION IS A PARTY WHERE ALL YOUR GUESTS come together to celebrate your new life as a married couple. It should reflect and complement the formality of your ceremony. The selection of a reception site will depend on its availability, price, proximity to the ceremony site, and the number of people it will accommodate.

RECEPTION SITE FEE

There are two basic types of reception sites. The first type charges a per person fee that includes the facility, food, tables, silverware, china, and so forth. Examples include hotels, restaurants, and catered yachts. The second type charges a room rental fee, and you are responsible for providing the food, beverages, linens, and possibly the tables and chairs. Examples include clubs, halls, parks, museums, and private homes.

The advantage of the first type is that almost everything is done for you. The disadvantage, however, is that your choices of food, china, and linen are limited. Usually you are not permitted to bring in an outside caterer, and must select from a predetermined menu.

Options: Private homes, gardens, hotels, clubs, restaurants, halls, parks, museums, yachts, and wineries are some of the more popular choices for receptions to help further personalize your big day.

Things to Consider: When comparing the costs of different locations, consider the rental fee, food, beverages, parking, gratuity, setup charges, in addition to the cost of rental equipment needed such as tables, chairs, canopies, and so forth. If you are planning an outdoor reception, be sure to have a backup site in case of rain.

Beware: Some hotels are known for double booking. A bride may reserve the largest or most elegant room in a hotel for her reception, only to find out later that the hotel took the liberty to book a more profitable event in the room she had reserved and moved her reception over to a smaller or less elegant room.

Also, be careful of hotels that book events too close together. You don't want your guests to wait outside while your room is being set up for the reception. And you don't want to be "forced out" before you are ready to leave because the hotel needs to arrange the room for the next reception. Get your rental hours and the name of your room in writing.

RECEPTION

Tips to Save Money: Since the cost of the reception is approximately 35% of the total cost of your wedding, you can save the most money by limiting your guest list. If you hire a wedding consultant, he or she may be able to cut your cake and save you the cake cutting fee. Check this out with your facility or caterer. Reception sites that charge a room rental fee may waive this fee if you meet minimum requirements on food and beverages consumed. Try to negotiate before you book the facility.

Price Range: $300 - $5,000

HORS D'OEUVRES

At receptions where a full meal is to be served, hors d'oeuvres may be offered to guests during the first hour of the reception. However, at a tea or cocktail reception, hors d'oeuvres will be the "main course."

Options: There are many options for hors d'oeuvres, depending on the formality of your reception, as well as the type of food to be served at the meal. Popular items are foods that can easily be picked up and eaten with one hand. Hors d'oeuvres may be set out on tables "buffet style" for guests to help themselves, or they may be passed around on trays by waiters and waitresses.

Things to Consider: When selecting hors d'oeuvres for your reception, consider whether heating or refrigeration will be available, and choose your food accordingly. When planning your menu, consider the time of day. You should select lighter hors d'oeuvres for a midday reception and heavier hors d'oeuvres for an evening reception.

Tips to Save Money: Pass around hors d'oeuvre trays during cocktail hour and serve a lighter meal. Avoid serving hors d'oeuvres that are labor intensive or that require expensive ingredients. Compare two or three caterers; there is a wide price range between caterers for the same food. And remember to compare the total cost of catering (main entrée plus hors d'oeuvres) when selecting a caterer. Consider serving hors d'oeuvres buffet style. Your guests will eat less this way than if waiters and waitresses are constantly serving them hors d'oeuvres.

Price Range: $3 - $20 per person

MAIN MEAL/CATERER

If your reception is going to be at a hotel, restaurant, or other facility that provides food, you will need to select a meal to serve your guests. Most of these facilities will have a predetermined menu from which to select your meal. If your reception is going to be in a facility that does not provide food, you will need to hire an outside caterer. The caterer will be responsible for preparing, cooking, and serving the food. The caterer will also be responsible for beverages and for cleaning up after the event. Before signing a contract, make sure you understand all the services the caterer will provide. Your contract should state the amount and type of food and beverages that will be served, the way in which they will be served, the number of servers who will be available, and the cost per food item or person.

Options: Food can be served either buffet style or as a sit-down meal. It should be chosen according to the time of day, year, and formality of the wedding. Although there are many main dishes to choose from, chicken and beef are the most popular selections for a large event. Ask your facility manager or caterer for their specialty. If you have a special type of food you would like to serve at your reception, select a facility or caterer who specializes in preparing it.

Things to Consider: When hiring a caterer, check to see if the location for your reception provides refrigeration and cooking equipment. If not, make sure your caterer is fully self-supported with portable refrigeration and heating equipment. A competent caterer will prepare much of the food in his or her own kitchen, and should provide an adequate staff of cooks, servers, and bartenders. Ask for references and look at photos from previous parties so you know how the food will be presented; or better yet, visit an event they are catering.

Beware: Avoid mayonnaise, cream sauces, or custard fillings if food must go unrefrigerated for any length of time.

Tips to Save Money: Give only 85 to 95 percent of your final guest count to your caterer or facility manager, depending on how certain you are that all of your guests who have responded will come. Chances are that several, if not many, of your guests will not show up. But if they do, your caterer should have enough food for all of them. This is especially true with buffet-style receptions, in which case the facility or caterer will charge extra for each additional guest. However, if you give a complete count of your guests to your caterer and some of them don't show up, you will still have to pay for their plates. If offering a buffet meal, have the catering staff serve the food onto guests' plates rather than allowing guests to serve themselves. This will help to regulate the amount of food consumed.

Select food that is not too time-consuming to prepare, or food that does not have expensive ingredients. Also, consider a brunch or early afternoon wedding so the reception will fall between meals, allowing you to serve hors d'oeuvres instead of a full meal. Or pass around trays of hors d'oeuvres during cocktail hour and choose a lighter meal.

Price Range: $20 - $100 per person

LIQUOR/BEVERAGES

Prices for liquor and beverages vary greatly, depending on the amount and brand of alcohol served. Traditionally, at least champagne or punch should be served to toast the couple.

RECEPTION

Options: White and red wines, scotch, vodka, gin, rum, and beer are the most popular alcoholic beverages. There are a number of options and variations for serving alcoholic beverages: a full open bar where you pay for your guests to drink as much as they wish; an open bar for the first hour, followed by a cash bar where guests pay for their own drinks; a cash bar only; beer and wine only; nonalcoholic beverages only; or any combination thereof. Sodas and fruit punch are popular nonalcoholic beverages served at receptions. And of course, don't forget coffee and/or tea is often served with the cake or other dessert options.

Things to Consider: If you plan to serve alcoholic beverages at a reception site that does not provide liquor, make sure your caterer has a license to serve alcohol, and that your reception site allows alcoholic beverages. If you plan to order your own alcohol, do so three or four weeks before the event. Those providing a no-host or "cash" bar, should consider notifying their guests so they know to bring cash with them. A simple line that says "No-Host Bar" on the reception card should suffice.

In selecting the type of alcohol to serve, consider the age and preference of your guests, the type of food that will be served, and the time of day your guests will be drinking.

On the average, you should allow one drink per person, per hour at the reception. A bottle of champagne will usually serve six glasses. Never serve liquor without some type of food. Use the following chart to plan your beverage needs:

Beverages	Amount based on 100 guests
Bourbon	3 Fifths
Gin	3 Fifths
Rum	2 Fifths
Scotch	4 Quarts
Vodka	5 Quarts
White Wine	2 Cases
Red Wine	1 Case
Champagne	3 Cases
Other	2 Cases each: Club Soda, Seltzer Water, Tonic Water, Ginger Ale, Cola, Beer

If you are hosting an open bar at a hotel or restaurant, ask the catering manager how they charge for liquor: by consumption or by number of bottles opened. Get this in writing before the event, and then ask for a full consumption report after the event.

Beware: In today's society, it is not uncommon for the hosts of a party to be held legally responsible for the conduct and safety of their guests. Keep this in mind when planning the quantity and type of beverages to serve. Also, be sure to remind your bartenders not to serve alcohol to minors.

Tips to Save Money: To keep beverage costs down, serve punch, wine, or nonalcoholic drinks only. If your caterer allows it, consider buying liquor from a wholesaler who will let you return unopened bottles. Also, avoid salty foods such as potato chips, pretzels, or ham. These foods will make your guests thirstier, so they will tend to drink more.

Host alcoholic beverages for the first hour, then go to a cash bar. Or host beer, wine, and soft drinks only, and have mixed drinks available on a cash basis. The bartending fee is often waived if you meet the minimum requirements on beverages consumed. For the toast, pass out champagne only to those guests who want it, not to everyone. Many people will make a toast with whatever they are currently drinking. Consider serving sparkling cider in place of champagne.

Omit waiters and waitresses. Instead, have an open bar in which your guests have to get their own drinks. Not only will you save on what you would have paid for this service, you will save on alcohol costs as well; people tend to drink almost twice as much if there are waiters and waitresses constantly asking them if they would like another drink and then bringing drinks to them.

Price Range: $8 - $35 per person

BARTENDING/BAR SETUP FEE

Some reception sites and caterers charge an extra fee for bartending and for setting up the bar.

Tips to Save Money: The bartending fee could be and often is waived if you meet a minimum requirement on beverages consumed. Try to negotiate this with your caterer prior to hiring him or her.

Price Range: $75 - $500

CORKAGE FEE

Many reception sites and caterers make money by marking up the food and alcohol they sell. You may wish to provide your own alcohol for a couple of reasons. First, it is more cost-effective. Second, you may want to serve an exotic wine or champagne that the reception site or caterer does not offer.

In either case, and if your reception site or caterer allows it, be prepared to pay a corkage fee. This is the fee for each bottle brought into the reception site and opened by a member of their staff.

Things to Consider: You need to consider whether the expenses saved after paying the corkage fee justify the hassle and liability of bringing in your own alcohol.

Price Range: $5 - $20 per bottle

FEE TO POUR COFFEE

In addition to corkage and cake cutting fees, some facilities also charge extra to pour the coffee served with the wedding cake.

Things to Consider: Again, when comparing the costs of various reception sites, don't forget to add up all the extra miscellaneous costs, such as the fee for pouring coffee.

Price Range: $0.25 - $1 per person

SERVICE PROVIDERS' MEALS

Things to Consider: It is considered a courtesy to feed your photographer, videographer, and any other "service provider" at the reception. Check options and prices with your caterer or reception site manager. Make sure you allocate a place for your service providers to eat. You may want them to eat with your guests, or you may prefer setting a place outside the main room for them to eat. Your service providers may be more comfortable with the latter.

Tips to Save Money: You don't need to feed your service providers the same meal as your guests. You can order sandwiches or another less expensive meal for them. If the meal is a buffet, there should be enough food left after all your guests have been served for your service providers to eat. Tell them they are welcome to eat after all your guests have been served. Be sure to discuss this with your catering manager.

Price Range: $10 - $30 per person

GRATUITY

It is customary to pay a gratuity fee to your caterer. The average gratuity is 15 to 20 percent of your food and beverage bill.

Tips to Save Money: Ask about these costs up front, and select your caterer or reception site accordingly.

Price Range: 15 - 25 percent of total food and beverage bill

PARTY FAVORS

Party favors are little gift items given to your guests as mementos of your wedding. They add a very special touch to your wedding and can become keepsakes for your guests.

Options: White matchboxes engraved with the couple's names and wedding date; cocktail napkins marked in the same way; individually wrapped and marked chocolates, almonds, or fine candy are popular party favors. Wine or champagne bottles marked with the bride and groom's names and wedding date on a personalized label also make great options. These come in a variety of sizes and can be purchased by the case.

If you can afford it, you may also consider porcelain or ceramic party favors. These can be custom-fired with your name and wedding date on them. And, a new idea that's gaining popularity among environmentally-conscientious couples is to present each guest with a tiny shoot of an endangered tree to be planted in honor of the bride and groom.

Things to Consider: Personalized favors need to be ordered several weeks in advance.

Price Range: $1 - $25 per person

ROSE PETALS/RICE

Rose petals or rice are traditionally tossed over the bride and groom as they leave the church after the ceremony or when they leave the reception. This tradition was initiated in the Middle Ages, when a handful of wheat was thrown over the bridal couple as a symbol of fertility. Rose petals are used to symbolize happiness, beauty, and prosperity.

RECEPTION

Options: Rose petals, rice, or confetti are often used. However, an environmentally correct alternative is to use flower or grass seeds. These can come wrapped in packages with the couple's names and wedding date printed on the front. Bubbles and sparklers have also become popular choices.

Things to Consider: Many clubs and hotels do not permit tossing rice or rose petals. Ask about your venue's policy.

Price Range: $0.35 - $2 per person

GIFT ATTENDANT

The gift attendant is responsible for watching over your gifts during the reception so that no one walks away with them. This is only necessary if your reception is held in a public area, such as a hotel or garden where strangers may be walking by. It is not proper to have a friend or family member take on this duty as he or she would not enjoy the reception. The gift attendant should also be responsible for transporting your gifts from the reception site to your car or bridal suite.

Tips to Save Money: Hire a young boy or girl from your neighborhood to watch over your gifts at the reception.

Price Range: $20 - $100

PARKING FEE/VALET SERVICES

Many reception sites such as hotels and restaurants charge for parking. It is customary, though not necessary, for the host of the wedding to pay this charge. At a large home reception, you should consider hiring a professional, qualified valet service if parking could be a problem. If so, make sure the valet service is fully insured.

Things to Consider: When comparing the costs of reception sites, don't forget to add the cost of parking to the total price.

Tips to Save Money: To avoid paying a valet service at a facility with limited parking, consider asking guests to park at a nearby church or school and hire a van to shuttle guests to your reception.

Price Range: $3 - $10 per car

GUEST ACCOMMODATION LIST

Make as many copies of this form as needed to accommodate the size of your guest list.

Name:

Arrival Date: Time:

Airline/Flight #:

Accommodation:

Departure Date: Time:

Airline/Flight #:

Phone:

Name:

Arrival Date: Time:

Airline/Flight #:

Accommodation:

Departure Date: Time:

Airline/Flight #:

Phone:

Name:

Arrival Date: Time:

Airline/Flight #:

Accommodation:

Departure Date: Time:

Airline/Flight #:

Phone:

Name:

Arrival Date: Time:

Airline/Flight #:

Accommodation:

Departure Date: Time:

Airline/Flight #:

Phone:

Name:

Arrival Date: Time:

Airline/Flight #:

Accommodation:

Departure Date: Time:

Airline/Flight #:

Phone:

Name:

Arrival Date: Time:

Airline/Flight #:

Accommodation:

Departure Date: Time:

Airline/Flight #:

Phone:

RECEPTION SITE COMPARISON CHART

QUESTIONS	POSSIBILITY 1	POSSIBILITY 2
What is the name of the reception site?		
What is the website and email of the reception site?		
What is the address of the reception site?		
What is the name and phone number of my contact person?		
What dates and times are available?		
What is the maximum number of guests for a seated reception?		
What is the maximum number of guests for a cocktail reception?		
What is the reception site fee?		
What is the price range for a seated lunch?		
What is the price range for a buffet lunch?		
What is the price range for a seated dinner?		
What is the price range for a buffet dinner?		
What is the corkage fee?		
What is the cake cutting fee?		
What is the ratio of servers to guests?		
How much time will be allotted for my reception?		
What music restrictions are there, if any?		
What alcohol restrictions are there, if any?		

POSSIBILITY 3	POSSIBILITY 4	POSSIBILITY 5	POSSIBILITY 6

QUESTIONS	POSSIBILITY 1	POSSIBILITY 2
Are there any restrictions for rice or rose petal tossing?		
What room and table decorations are available?		
Is a changing room available?		
Is there handicap accessibility?		
Is a dance floor included in the site fee?		
Are tables, chairs, and linens included in the site fee?		
Are outside caterers allowed?		
Are kitchen facilities available for outside caterers?		
Does the facility have full liability insurance?		
What perks or giveaways are offered?		
How many parking spaces are available for my wedding party?		
How many parking spaces are available for my guests?		
What is the cost for parking, if any?		
What is the cost for sleeping rooms, if available?		
What is the payment policy?		
What is the cancellation policy?		

POSSIBILITY 3	POSSIBILITY 4	POSSIBILITY 5	POSSIBILITY 6

RECEPTION SITE INFORMATION SHEET

RECEPTION SITE:

Site Coordinator: _____ Cost: _____

Website: _____

Email: _____

Phone Number: _____

Address: _____

City: _____ State: _____ Zip Code: _____

Name of Room: Capacity: _____

Date Confirmed: _____ Confirm Head Count By: _____

Beginning Time: _____ Ending Time: _____

Cocktails/Hors d'Oeuvres Time: _____ Meal Time: _____

Color of Linens: _____ Color of Napkins: _____

Total Cost: _____

Deposit: _____ Date: _____

Balance: _____ Date Due: _____

Cancellation Policy: _____

EQUIPMENT INCLUDES:

❑ Tables ❑ Chairs ❑ Linens ❑ Tableware
❑ Barware ❑ Heaters ❑ Electric Outlet ❑ Musical Instruments

SERVICE INCLUDES:

❑ Waiters ❑ Bartenders ❑ Valet ❑ Main Meal
❑ Clean Up ❑ Setup ❑ Security ❑ Free Parking

CATERER:

Contact Person: Cost Per Person:

Website:

Email:

Phone Number:

Address:

City: State: Zip Code:

Confirmed Date: Confirm Head Count By:

Arrival Time: Departure Time:

Cocktails/Hors d'Oeuvres Time: Meal Time:

Color of Linens: Color of Napkins:

Total Cost:

Deposit: Date:

Balance: Date Due:

Cancellation Policy:

EQUIPMENT INCLUDES:

❑ Tables   ❑ Chairs   ❑ Linens   ❑ Tableware
❑ Barware   ❑ Heaters   ❑ Lighting   ❑ Candles

SERVICE INCLUDES:

❑ Waiters   ❑ Bartenders   ❑ Setup   ❑ Clean Up
❑ Security   ❑ Hors d'Oeuvres ❑ Buffet Meal   ❑ Seated Meal
❑ Cocktails   ❑ Champagne   ❑ Wine   ❑ Beer
❑ Punch   ❑ Soft Drinks   ❑ Coffee/Tea   ❑ Cake

TABLE SEATING ARRANGEMENTS

Complete this form only after finalizing your guest list. Make as many copies of this form as needed.

HEAD TABLE	BRIDE'S FAMILY TABLE	GROOM'S FAMILY TABLE
_____	_____	_____
_____	_____	_____
_____	_____	_____
_____	_____	_____
_____	_____	_____
_____	_____	_____
_____	_____	_____
_____	_____	_____

• TABLE __	• TABLE __	• TABLE __
_____	_____	_____
_____	_____	_____
_____	_____	_____
_____	_____	_____
_____	_____	_____
_____	_____	_____
_____	_____	_____
_____	_____	_____

• TABLE __	• TABLE __	• TABLE __
_____	_____	_____
_____	_____	_____
_____	_____	_____
_____	_____	_____
_____	_____	_____
_____	_____	_____
_____	_____	_____

TABLE SEATING ARRANGEMENTS

Complete this form only after finalizing your guest list. Make as many copies of this form as needed.

• TABLE __

_____
_____
_____
_____
_____
_____
_____
_____

• TABLE __

_____
_____
_____
_____
_____
_____
_____
_____

• TABLE __

_____
_____
_____
_____
_____
_____
_____
_____

• TABLE __

_____
_____
_____
_____
_____
_____
_____
_____

• TABLE __

_____
_____
_____
_____
_____
_____
_____
_____

• TABLE __

_____
_____
_____
_____
_____
_____
_____
_____

• TABLE __

_____
_____
_____
_____
_____
_____
_____
_____

• TABLE __

_____
_____
_____
_____
_____
_____
_____
_____

• TABLE __

_____
_____
_____
_____
_____
_____
_____
_____

LIQUOR ORDER FORM

LIQUOR VENDOR: _____   Date Ordered: _____

Salesperson: _____   Phone Number: _____

Website: _____

Email: _____

Address: _____

City: _____   State: _____   Zip Code: _____

Cost: _____

Delivered By: _____   Delivery Date: _____

TYPE OF LIQUOR	**# of Bottles Needed**	**Price**

PARTY FAVORS COMPARISON CHART

Party favors might include matchbooks, personalized wine bottles, chocolates, candies, or frames.

TYPE OF FAVOR	Website/Company	Quantity	Price

CATERER COMPARISON CHART

QUESTIONS	POSSIBILITY 1	POSSIBILITY 2
What is the name of the caterer?		
What is the website and email of the caterer?		
What is the address of the caterer?		
What is the name and phone number of my contact person?		
How many years have you been in business?		
What percentage of your business is dedicated to receptions?		
Do you have liability insurance/license to serve alcohol?		
When is the final head count needed?		
What is your ratio of servers to guests?		
How do your servers dress for wedding receptions?		
What is your price range for a seated lunch/buffet lunch?		
What is your price range for a seated/buffet dinner?		
How much gratuity is expected?		
What is your specialty?		
What is your cake cutting fee?		
What is your bartending fee?		
What is your fee to clean up after the reception?		
What is your payment policy?		
What is your cancellation policy?		

POSSIBILITY 3	POSSIBILITY 4	POSSIBILITY 5	POSSIBILITY 6

MENU WORKSHEET

HORS D'OEUVRES:

_____

_____

_____

SALADS/APPETIZERS:

_____

_____

_____

SOUPS:

_____

_____

_____

MAIN ENTRÉE:

_____

_____

_____

DESSERTS:

_____

_____

_____

WEDDING CAKE:

_____

_____

_____

MUSIC
& BAKERY

Karen French

MUSIC

CEREMONY MUSIC IS THE MUSIC PLAYED DURING the prelude, processional, ceremony, recessional, and postlude. Prelude music is played while guests are being seated, 15 to 30 minutes before the ceremony begins. Processional music is played as the wedding party enters the ceremony site. Recessional music is played as the wedding party leaves the ceremony site. Postlude music is played while the guests leave the ceremony site.

CEREMONY MUSIC

Options: The most traditional musical instrument for wedding ceremonies is the organ. However, guitars, pianos, flutes, harps, and violins are also popular today.

Popular selections for a Christian wedding:

"Trumpet Voluntary" by Purcell
"The Bridal Chorus" by Wagner
"Wedding March" by Mendelssohn
"Postlude in G Major" by Handel
"Canon in D Major" by Pachelbel
"Adagio in A Minor" by Bach

Popular selections for a Jewish wedding:

"Erev Shel Shoshanim"
"Erev Ba"
"Hana' Ava Babanot"

Things to Consider: Music may or may not be included as part of the ceremony site fee. Be sure to check with your ceremony site about restrictions pertaining to music and the availability of musical instruments for your use. Discuss the selection of ceremony music with your officiant and musicians. Make sure the musicians know how to play the selections you request.

When selecting ceremony music, keep in mind the formality of your wedding, your religious affiliation, and the length of the ceremony. Also consider the location and time of day. If the ceremony is outside where there may be other noises such as traffic, wind, or people's voices, or if a large number of guests will be attending your ceremony, consider having the music, your officiant, and your vows amplified. Make sure there are electrical outlets close to where the instruments will be set up.

Tips to Save Money: Hire student musicians from your local university or high school. Ask a friend to sing or play at your ceremony; they will be honored. If you're planning to hire a band for your reception, consider hiring a scaled-down version of the same band to play at your ceremony, such as a flute trio, guitar, and vocals.

Price Range: $100 - $900

MUSIC

RECEPTION MUSIC

Music is a major part of your reception, and should be planned carefully. Music helps create the atmosphere of your wedding. Special songs will make your reception unique. When you select music for your reception, keep in mind the age and musical preference of your guests, your budget, and any restrictions that the reception site may have. Bands and musicians are typically more expensive than DJs.

Options: There are many options for reception music: you can hire a DJ, a band, an orchestra, or any combination of one or more instruments and vocalists.

Things to Consider: Hire an entertainment agency that can help you choose a reliable DJ or band that has experience performing at weddings. If you want your musician to act as a master of ceremonies, make sure he or she has a complete timeline for your reception in order to announce the various events, including the toasts, first dance, and cutting of the cake. Consider watching your musicians perform at another event before booking their services.

If you need a large variety of music to satisfy all your guests, hiring a DJ is a great option. A professional DJ can play any type of music, and may even offer a light show. Make sure you give him or her a list of the songs you want played at your reception and the sequence in which you want them played.

Tips to Save Money: You will probably get a better price if you hire a band or DJ directly than if you hire them through an entertainment agency. Check the music department of local colleges and universities for names of student musicians and DJs. You may be able to hire a student for a fraction of the price of a professional musician or DJ. A DJ is typically less expensive than a "live" musician. Some facilities have contracts with certain DJs, and you may be able to save money by hiring one of them.

Price Range: $500 - $5,000

WHEN	Selection	Composer	Played By
Prelude 1			
Prelude 2			
Prelude 3			
Processional			
Bride's Processional			
Ceremony 1			
Ceremony 2			
Ceremony 3			
Recessional			
Postlude			
Other:			
Other:			
Other:			
Other:			
Other:			
Other:			
Other:			

CEREMONY MUSIC COMPARISON CHART

QUESTIONS	POSSIBILITY 1	POSSIBILITY 2
What is the name of the musician or band?		
What is the website and email of the musician or band?		
What is the address of the musician or band?		
What is the name and phone number of my contact person?		
How many years of professional experience do you have?		
What percentage of your business is dedicated to weddings?		
Are you the person who will perform at my wedding?		
What instrument(s) do you play?		
What type of music do you specialize in?		
What are your hourly fees?		
What is the cost of a soloist?		
What is the cost of a duet?		
What is the cost of a trio?		
What is the cost of a quartet?		
How would you dress for my wedding?		
Do you have liability insurance?		
Do you have a cordless microphone?		
What are your payment and cancellation policies?		

CEREMONY MUSIC COMPARISON CHART

POSSIBILITY 3	POSSIBILITY 4	POSSIBILITY 5	POSSIBILITY 6

RECEPTION MUSIC COMPARISON CHART

QUESTIONS	POSSIBILITY 1	POSSIBILITY 2
What is the name of the musician, band, or DJ?		
What is the website and email of the musician, band, or DJ?		
What is the address of the musician, band, or DJ?		
What is the name and phone number of my contact person?		
How many years of professional experience do you have?		
What percentage of your business is dedicated to receptions?		
How many people are in your band?		
What type of music do you specialize in?		
What type of sound system do you have?		
Can you act as a master of ceremonies? How do you dress for weddings?		
Can you provide a light show?		
Do you have a cordless microphone?		
How many breaks do you take? How long are they?		
Do you play recorded music during breaks?		
Do you have liability insurance?		
What are your fees for a 4-hour reception?		
What is your cost for each additional hour?		

POSSIBILITY 3	POSSIBILITY 4	POSSIBILITY 5	POSSIBILITY 6

RECEPTION MUSIC SELECTIONS

Make a copy of this form and give it to your musicians.

WHEN	Selection	Songwriter	Played By
Receiving Line			
During Hors d'Oeuvres			
During Dinner			
First Dance			
Second Dance			
Third Dance			
Bouquet Toss			
Garter Removal			
Cutting of the Cake			
Last Dance			
Couple Leaving			
Other:			
Other:			
Other:			
Other:			
Other:			
Other:			

BAKERY

WHEN ORDERING A WEDDING CAKE, YOU WILL HAVE TO DECIDE not only on a flavor, but also on size, shape, and color. How many tiers do you want? What flavors? What kind of icing or decorations? You are best off ordering from a bakery that specializes in wedding cakes. Ask to see photographs of other wedding cakes your baker has created, and by all means, ask for a tasting!

WEDDING CAKE

Options: Choose from round, square, heart-shaped, hexagonal, petal, or topsy-turvey tiers. The most common flavors are chocolate, carrot, lemon, red velvet, and white cakes. Be creative by adding filling to your cake, such as mousse, fruit, or chocolate. You can choose different flavors for different tiers. In addition to flavor, size, and cost, consider decoration and spoilage.

Things to Consider: Price, workmanship, quality, and taste vary considerably from baker to baker. Don't forget to think about styles and accessories, as well as the possibility of spoilage (sugar keeps longer than cream frostings). The cake should be beautifully displayed on its own table decorated with flowers or greenery. Ask if the baker, caterer, or reception site manager can provide you with a pretty, decorative cake knife. If not, you will need to purchase or rent one.

When determining the size of the cake, don't forget that you'll be saving the top tier for your first anniversary. This top tier should be removed before the cake is cut, wrapped in several layers of plastic wrap or put inside a plastic container. Keep it frozen until you celebrate your first anniversary.

Tips to Save Money: Some bakers have setup and delivery fees, and others don't. Check for individuals who bake from their homes. They are usually more reasonable, but you should check with your local health department before hiring one of these at-home bakers. Also, your caterer may have contracts with local bakeries, and can pass on savings to you. Some bakeries require a deposit on columns and plates; other bakeries use disposable columns and plates, saving you the rental fee and the hassle of returning these items.

Price Range: $2 - $12 per piece

BAKERY

GROOM'S CAKE

The groom's cake is an old Southern tradition. This cake was originally cut and distributed to guests in little white boxes engraved with the bride and groom's names. Today the groom's cake, if offered, is cut and served along with the wedding cake.

Options: Usually a chocolate cake decorated with fruit.

Tips to Save Money: Because of its cost and the labor involved in cutting and distribution, very few people opt for this custom anymore.

Price Range: $1 - $2 per piece

CAKE DELIVERY/SETUP FEE

This is the fee charged by bakers to deliver and set up your wedding cake at the reception site. It usually includes a deposit on the cake pillars and plate, which will be refunded upon their return to the baker.

Tips to Save Money: Enlist a friend or family member to get a quick lesson on how to set up your cake. Have them pick it up and set it up the day of your wedding, then have the florist decorate the cake and/or cake table with flowers and greenery.

Price Range: $40 - $100

CAKE CUTTING FEE

Most reception sites and caterers charge a fee for each slice of cake they cut if the cake is brought in from an outside bakery. This fee will probably shock you. It is simply their way of enticing you to order the cake through them. Unfortunately, many caterers will not allow a member of your party to cut the cake.

Tips to Save Money: Many hotels and restaurants include a dessert in the cost of their meal packages. If you forgo this option and substitute your cake as the dessert, they may be willing to waive the cake cutting fee. Be sure to ask!

Price Range: $1 - $3 per person

CAKE TOPPER

The bride's cake is often topped with traditional "cake toppers," such as figurines designed to look like the couple, bells, love birds, flowers, or your initials.

Things to Consider: Some porcelain and other heavier cake toppers need to be anchored down into the cake. If you're planning to use a cake topper other than flowers, be sure to discuss this with your baker.

Tips to Save Money: Borrow a cake topper from a friend or a family member as your "something borrowed," an age-old wedding tradition.

Price Range: $20 - $150

CAKE KNIFE/TOASTING GLASSES

Your cake knife and toasting glasses should complement your overall setting; these items will bring you happy memories of your wedding day every time you use them. The cake knife is used to cut the cake at the reception. The bride usually cuts the first two slices of the wedding cake with the groom's hand placed over hers. The groom feeds the bride first. Then, the bride feeds the groom. This tradition makes beautiful wedding photographs.

You will need toasting glasses to toast each other after cutting the cake. They are usually decorated with ribbons or flowers, and kept near the cake. This tradition is also a great opportunity for photos.

Things to Consider: Consider having your initials and wedding date engraved on your wedding knife as a memento. Think about purchasing crystal or silver toasting glasses as a keepsake of your wedding. Have your florist decorate your knife and toasting glasses with flowers or ribbons.

Tips to Save Money: Borrow your cake knife or toasting glasses from a friend or family member as your "something borrowed." Or, use the reception facility's glasses and knife, and decorate them with flowers or ribbon.

Price Range: $15 - $120 for knife; $10 - $100 for toasting glasses

BAKERY COMPARISON CHART

QUESTIONS	POSSIBILITY 1	POSSIBILITY 2
What is the name of the bakery?		
What is the bakery's website and email?		
What is the address of the bakery?		
What is the name and phone number of my contact person?		
How many years have you been making wedding cakes?		
What are your wedding cake specialties?		
Do you offer free tasting of your wedding cakes?		
Are your wedding cakes fresh or frozen?		
How far in advance should I order my cake?		
Can you make a groom's cake?		
Do you lend, rent, or sell cake knives?		
What is the cost per serving of my desired cake?		
What is your cake pillar and plate rental fee, if any?		
Is this fee refundable upon the return of these items?		
When must these items be returned?		
What is your cake delivery and setup fee?		
What is your payment policy?		
What is your cancellation policy?		

POSSIBILITY 3	POSSIBILITY 4	POSSIBILITY 5	POSSIBILITY 6

CAKE TASTING CHART

BAKERY OPTION 1

Company Name: _____ Contact Person: _____

Flavor	Price Per Slice	Notes
1)	$	
2)	$	
3)	$	

BAKERY OPTION 2

Company Name: _____ Contact Person: _____

Flavor	Price Per Slice	Notes
1)	$	
2)	$	
3)	$	

BAKERY OPTION 3

Company Name: _____ Contact Person: _____

Flavor	Price Per Slice	Notes
1)	$	
2)	$	
3)	$	

FLOWERS & DECORATIONS

Karen French

FLOWERS

FLOWERS ADD BEAUTY, FRAGRANCE, AND COLOR TO YOUR WEDDING. Like everything else, flowers should fit your overall style and color scheme. Flowers make vibrant decorations and add personal touches to the main altar, aisle, pews, guest tables, reception site, wedding party attire, cake table, and much more. Choosing the most beautiful flowers suiting your theme and season is an exciting aspect of wedding planning.

BRIDE'S BOUQUET

The bridal bouquet is one of the most important elements of the bride's attire and deserves special attention. Start by selecting the color and shape of the bouquet. The bridal bouquet should be carried low enough so that all the intricate details of your gown are visible.

Options: There are many colors, scents, sizes, shapes, and styles of bouquets to choose from. Popular styles are the cascade, cluster, contemporary, and hand-tied garden bouquets. The traditional bridal bouquet is made of white flowers. Stephanotis, gardenias, white roses, orchids, and lilies of the valley are popular choices for an all-white bouquet.

If you prefer a colorful bouquet, you may want to consider using roses, tulips, stock, peonies, freesia, and gerbera, which come in a wide variety of colors. Using scented flowers in your bouquet will evoke memories of your wedding day whenever you smell them in the future. Popular fragrant flowers are gardenias, freesia, stephanotis, bouvardia, and narcissus. Select flowers that are in season to assure availability.

Things to Consider: Your flowers should complement the season, your gown, your color scheme, your attendants' attire, and the style and formality of your wedding. If you have a favorite flower, build your bouquet around it, and include it in all your arrangements. Some flowers carry centuries of symbolism. Consider stephanotis—tradition regards it as the bridal flower for good luck! Pimpernel signifies change; white flowers radiate innocence; forget-me-nots indicate true love; and ivy stands for friendship, fidelity, and matrimony, the three essentials for a happy marriage.

No flower, however, has as much symbolism for brides as the orange blossom, having at least 700 years of nuptial history. Its unusual ability to simultaneously produce flowers and fruit symbolizes the fusion of beauty, personality, and fertility.

FLOWERS

Whatever flowers you select, final arrangements should be made well in advance of your wedding date to ensure availability. Confirm your final order and delivery time a few days before the wedding. Have the flowers delivered before the photographer arrives so that you can include them in your pre-ceremony photos.

In determining the size of your bouquet, consider your gown and your overall stature. Carry a smaller bouquet if you're petite or if your gown is fairly ornate. A long, cascading bouquet complements a fairly simple gown or a tall or larger bride. Arm bouquets look best when resting naturally in the crook of your arm.

For a natural, fresh-picked look, have your florist put together a cluster of flowers tied together with a ribbon. For a Victorian appeal, carry a nosegay or a basket filled with flowers. Or carry a Bible or other family heirloom decorated with just a few flowers. For a contemporary look, you may want to consider carrying an arrangement of calla lilies or other long-stemmed flower over your arm. For a dramatic statement, carry a single stem of your favorite flower!

Beware: If your bouquet includes delicate flowers that will not withstand hours of heat or a lack of water, make sure your florist uses a bouquet holder to keep them fresh. If you want to carry fresh-cut stems without a bouquet holder, make sure the flowers you select are hardy enough to go without water for the duration of your ceremony and reception.

Tips to Save Money: The cost of some flowers may be significantly higher during their off-season. Try to select flowers that are in bloom and plentiful at the time of your wedding. Avoid exotic, out-of-season flowers. Allow your florist to emphasize your colors using more reasonable, seasonal flowers to achieve your overall look. If you have a favorite flower that is costly or out of season, consider using silk for that one flower.

Avoid scheduling your wedding on holidays such as Valentine's Day and Mother's Day when the price of flowers is higher. Because every attendant will carry or wear flowers, consider keeping the size of your wedding party small to accommodate your floral budget.

Price Range: $75 - $400

TOSSING BOUQUET

If you want to preserve your bridal bouquet, consider having your florist make a smaller, less expensive bouquet specifically for tossing. This will be the bouquet you toss to your single female friends toward the end of the reception. Tradition has it that the woman who catches the bouquet is the next to be married. Have your florist include a few sprigs of fresh ivy in the tossing bouquet to symbolize friendship and fidelity.

Tips to Save Money: Use the floral cake topper or guest book table "tickler bouquet" as the tossing bouquet. Or omit the tossing bouquet altogether and simply toss your bridal bouquet.

Price Range: $20 - $100

MAID OF HONOR'S BOUQUET

The maid of honor's bouquet can be somewhat larger or of a different color than the rest of the bridesmaids' bouquets. This will help to set her apart from the others.

Price Range: $25 - $100

BRIDESMAIDS' BOUQUETS

The bridesmaids' bouquets should complement the bridal bouquet, but are generally smaller in size. The size and color should coordinate with the bridesmaids' dresses and the overall style of the wedding. Bridesmaids' bouquets are usually identical.

Options: To personalize your bridesmaids' bouquets, insert a different flower in each of their bouquets to make a statement. For example, if one of your bridesmaids has been sad, give her a lily of the valley to symbolize the return of happiness. To tell a friend that you admire her, insert yellow jasmine. A pansy will let your friend know that you are thinking of her.

Things to Consider: Choose a bouquet style (cascade, cluster, contemporary, hand-tied) that complements the formality of your wedding and the height of your attendants. If your bridesmaids will be wearing floral print dresses, select flowers that complement the floral print.

Tips to Save Money: Have your attendants carry a single stemmed rose, lily, or another suitable flower for an elegant look that also saves money.

Price Range: $25 - $100

MAID OF HONOR/BRIDESMAIDS' HAIRPIECE

For a garden look, have your maid of honor and bridesmaids wear garlands of flowers in their hair. Provide your maid of honor with a slightly different color or variety of flower to set her apart from the others.

Options: You may consider using artificial flowers for the hairpieces as long as they are in keeping with the flowers carried by members of the bridal party. Since it is not always easy to find good artificial blooms, other types of hairpieces may be more satisfactory, durable, and attractive.

Things to Consider: Flowers used for hairpieces must be sturdy and have long lives.

Price Range: $8 - $100

FLOWER GIRL'S HAIRPIECE

Flower girls often wear a wreath of flowers as a hairpiece.

Options: This is another place where artificial flowers may be used, but they must complement the flowers carried by members of the bridal party. Since it is not always easy to find good artificial blooms, other types of hairpieces may be more satisfactory, durable, and attractive.

Things to Consider: If the flowers used for the hairpiece are not a sturdy and long-lived variety, a ribbon, bow, or hat might be a safer choice.

Price Range: $8 - $75

BRIDE'S GOING AWAY CORSAGE

You may want to consider wearing a corsage on your going away outfit. This makes for pretty photos as you and your new husband leave the reception for your honeymoon. Have your florist create a corsage which echoes the beauty of your bouquet.

Beware: Put a protective shield under lilies when using them as a corsage, as their anthers will easily stain fabric. Be careful when using alstroemeria as a corsage, as its sap can be harmful if it enters the human bloodstream.

Tips to Save Money: Ask your florist if he or she can design your bridal bouquet in such a way that the center flowers may be removed and worn as a corsage. Or omit this corsage altogether.

Price Range: $10 - $50

FAMILY MEMBERS' CORSAGES

The groom is responsible for providing flowers for his mother, the bride's mother, and the grandmothers. The officiant, if female, may also be given a corsage to reflect her important role in the ceremony. The corsages don't have to be identical, but they should be coordinated with the color of their dresses.

Options: The groom may order flowers that can be pinned to a pocketbook or worn around a wrist. He should ask which style the women prefer, and if a particular color is needed to coordinate with their dresses. Gardenias, camellias, white orchids, or cymbidium orchids are excellent choices for corsages, as they go well with any outfit.

Things to Consider: The groom may also want to consider ordering corsages for other close family members, such as sisters and aunts. This will add a little to your floral expenses but will make these female family members feel more included in your wedding, and will let guests know that they are related to the bride and groom. However, keep in mind that some women do not like to wear corsages, so the groom should check with the people involved before ordering the flowers.

Beware: Put a protective shield under lilies when using them as corsages, as their anthers will easily stain fabric. Be careful when using alstroemeria as corsages, as the sap can be harmful if it enters the human bloodstream.

Tips to Save Money: Ask your florist to recommend reasonable flowers for corsages. Dendrobium orchids are reasonable and make lovely corsages.

Price Range: $10 - $35

GROOM'S BOUTONNIERE

The groom wears his boutonniere on the left lapel, nearest to his heart.

Options: Boutonnieres are generally a single blossom such as a rosebud, stephanotis, freesia, or a miniature carnation. If a rosebud is used for the wedding party, have the groom wear two, or add a sprig of baby's breath to differentiate him from the ushers.

Things to Consider: You may use a small cluster of flowers instead of a single bloom for the groom's boutonniere.

Beware: Be careful when using alstroemeria as a boutonniere. The sap can be dangerous if it enters the human bloodstream.

Tips to Save Money: Use mini-carnations rather than roses.

Price Range: $4 - $25

FLOWERS

USHERS/OTHER FAMILY MEMBERS' BOUTONNIERES

The groom gives each man in his wedding party a boutonniere to wear on his left lapel. The offici-ant, if male, may also be given a boutonniere to reflect his important role in the ceremony. The ring bearer may or may not wear a boutonniere, depending on his outfit. A boutonniere is more appro-priate on a tuxedo than on an outfit that includes knickers and knee socks.

Options: Generally, a single blossom such as a rosebud, freesia, or miniature carnation is used as a boutonniere.

Things to Consider: The groom should also consider ordering boutonnieres for other close family members such as fathers, grandfathers, and brothers. This will add a little to your floral expenses, but will make these male family members feel more included in your wedding, and will let guests know that they are related to the bride and groom.

Beware: Be careful when using alstroemeria as boutonnieres, as its sap can be harmful if it enters the human bloodstream.

Tips to Save Money: Use mini-carnations rather than roses.

Price Range: $3 - $15

MAIN ALTAR

The purpose of flowers at the main altar is to direct the guests' visual attention toward the front of the church or synagogue and to the bridal couple. Therefore, they must be seen by guests seated in the back. The flowers for the ceremony site can be as elaborate or as simple as you wish. Your officiant's advice, or that of the altar guild or florist, can be most helpful in choosing flowers for the altar.

Options: If your ceremony is outside, decorate the arch, gazebo, or alternative structure serving as the altar with flowers or greenery. In a Jewish ceremony, vows are said under a Chuppah, which is placed at the altar and covered with greens and fresh flowers.

Things to Consider: In choosing floral accents, consider the décor of your ceremony site. Some churches and synagogues are ornate enough that they don't need extra flowers. Too many arrange-ments would get lost in the architectural splendor. Select a few dramatic showpieces that will complement the existing décor. Be sure to ask if there are any restrictions on flowers at the church or synagogue. Remember, decorations should be determined by the size and style of the building, the formality of the wedding, the preferences of the couple, the cost, and the regulations of the particular site.

Tips to Save Money: Decorate the ceremony site with greenery only. Candlelight and greenery are elegant in and of themselves. Use greenery and flowers from your garden. Have your ceremony outside in a beautiful garden or on the beach so that you're surrounded by natural splendor.

Price Range: $50 - $3,000

ALTAR CANDELABRA

In a candlelight ceremony, the candelabra may be decorated with flowers or greens for a dramatic effect.

Options: Ivy is a great option, as it can be easily twined around the candelabra.

Price Range: $50 - $200

AISLE PEWS

Flowers, candles, or ribbons are often used to mark the aisle pews and add color.

Options: A cluster of flowers, a cascade of greens, or a combination of flowers and ribbons are all popular choices. Candles with adorning greenery add an elegant touch.

Things to Consider: Use hardy flowers that can tolerate being handled as pew ornaments. Gardenias and camellias, for example, are too sensitive to last long.

Beware: Avoid using allium in your aisle pew decorations, as they have an odor of onions.

Tips to Save Money: It is not necessary to decorate all of the aisle pews, or any at all. To save money, decorate only the reserved family pews, or every second or third pew.

Price Range: $5 - $75

RECEPTION SITE

Flowers add beauty, fragrance, and color to your reception. Flowers for the reception, like everything else, should fit your overall style and color scheme. Flowers can help transform a stark reception hall into a warm, inviting, and colorful room.

FLOWERS

Things to Consider: You can rent indoor plants or small trees to give your reception a garden-like atmosphere. Decorate them with twinkle lights to achieve a magical effect.

Tips to Save Money: You can save money by taking flowers from the ceremony to the reception site for decorations. However, you must coordinate this move carefully to avoid having your guests enter an undecorated reception room. Use greenery rather than flowers to fill large areas. Trees and garlands of ivy can give a dramatic impact for little money. Use greenery and flowers from your yard. Have your reception outside in a beautiful garden to take advantage of the naturally stunning environment. Water-side locations also make for beautiful ambiances.

Price Range: $300 - $3,000

HEAD TABLE

The head table is where the wedding party will sit during the reception. This important spot should be decorated with a larger or more dramatic centerpiece than the guest tables.

Things to Consider: Consider using a different color or style of arrangement to set the head table apart from the other tables.

Beware: Avoid using highly fragrant flowers, such as narcissus, on tables where food is being served or eaten, as their fragrance may conflict with other aromas.

Tips to Save Money: Decorate the head table with the bridal and attendants' bouquets.

Price Range: $100 - $600

GUEST TABLES

At a reception where guests are seated, a small flower arrangement may be placed on each table.

Things to Consider: The arrangements should complement the table linens and the size of the table, and should be kept low enough so as not to hinder conversation among guests seated across from each other.

Beware: Avoid using highly fragrant flowers, like narcissus, on tables where food is being served or eaten. Their fragrance may conflict with other aromas.

Tips to Save Money: To keep the cost down and for less formal receptions, use small potted flowering plants placed in white baskets, or consider using dried or silk arrangements that you can make yourself and give later as gifts. Or, place a wreath of greenery entwined with colored ribbon in the center of each table. Use a different colored ribbon at each table and assign your guests to tables by ribbon color instead of number.

Price Range: $10 - $100

BUFFET TABLE

If buffet tables are used, have some type of floral arrangement on the tables to add color and beauty to your display of food.

Options: Whole fruits and bunches of berries offer a variety of design possibilities. Figs add a festive touch. Pineapples are a sign of hospitality. Vegetables offer an endless array of colors and shapes with which to decorate. Herbs are yet another choice in decorating. A mixture of rosemary and mint combined with scented geraniums creates elegant and unique table décor.

Things to Consider: Depending on the size of the table, place one or two arrangements at each side.

Beware: Avoid placing certain flowers, such as carnations, snapdragons, or the star of Bethlehem next to buffet displays of fruits or vegetables, as they are extremely sensitive to the gasses emitted by these foods.

Price Range: $50 - $500

PUNCH TABLE

Put an assortment of greens or a small arrangement of flowers at the punch table. See "Buffet Table."

Price Range: $10 - $100

CAKE TABLE

The wedding cake is often the central location at the reception. Decorate the cake table with flowers.

Tips to Save Money: Have your bridesmaids place their bouquets on the cake table during the reception, or decorate the cake topper only and surround the base with greenery and a few loose flowers.

Price Range: $30 - $300

FLOWERS

CAKE

Flowers are a beautiful addition to a wedding cake, and are commonly seen spilling out between the cake tiers.

Things to Consider: Use only nonpoisonous flowers, and have your florist (not the caterer) design the floral decorations for your cake. A florist will be able to blend the cake decorations into your overall floral theme.

Price Range: $20 - $100

CAKE KNIFE

Decorate your cake knife with a white satin ribbon and flowers.

Things to Consider: Consider engraving the cake knife with your names and wedding date.

Price Range: $5 - $35

TOASTING GLASSES

Tie small flowers with white ribbon onto the stems of your champagne glasses. These wedding accessories deserve a special floral touch since they will most likely be included in your special photographs.

Things to Consider: Consider engraving your toasting glasses with your names and wedding date.

Price Range: $10 - $35

FLORAL DELIVERY/SETUP

Most florists charge a fee to deliver flowers to the ceremony and reception sites, as well as to arrange them on-site.

Things to Consider: Make sure your florist knows where your sites are and what time to arrive in order to set up.

Price Range: $25 - $200

BRIDE'S BOUQUET

Color Scheme: _____

Style: _____

Flowers: _____

_____

_____

Greenery: _____

Other (Ribbons, etc.): _____

MAID OF HONOR'S BOUQUET

Color Scheme: _____

Style: _____

Flowers: _____

_____

_____

Greenery: _____

Other (Ribbons, etc.): _____

BRIDESMAIDS' BOUQUETS

Color Scheme: _____

Style: _____

Flowers: _____

_____

_____

Greenery: _____

Other (Ribbons, etc.): _____

BOUQUETS AND FLOWERS

FLOWER GIRL'S BOUQUET

Color Scheme:

Style:

Flowers:

Greenery:

Other (Ribbons, etc.):

OTHER

Groom's Boutonniere:

Ushers and Other Family Members' Boutonnieres:

Mother of the Bride's Corsage:

Mother of the Groom's Corsage:

Altar or Chuppah:

Steps to Altar or Chuppah:

OTHER

Pews:

Entrance to the Ceremony:

Entrance to the Reception:

Receiving Line:

Head Table:

Parents' Table:

Guest Table:

Cake Table:

Serving Table (Buffet, Dessert):

Gift Table:

FLORIST COMPARISON CHART

QUESTIONS	POSSIBILITY 1	POSSIBILITY 2
What is the name of the florist?		
What is the website and email of the florist?		
What is the address of the florist?		
What are your business hours?		
What is the name and phone number of my contact person?		
How many years of professional floral experience do you have?		
What percentage of your business is dedicated to weddings?		
Do you have access to out-of-season flowers?		
Will you visit my wedding sites to make floral recommendations?		
Can you preserve my bridal bouquet?		
Do you rent vases and candleholders?		
Can you provide silk flowers?		
What is the cost of the desired bridal bouquet?		
What is the cost of the desired boutonniere?		
What is the cost of the desired corsage?		
Do you have liability insurance?		
What are your delivery/setup fees?		
What is your payment/cancellation policy?		

POSSIBILITY 3	POSSIBILITY 4	POSSIBILITY 5	POSSIBILITY 6

FLOWERS AND THEIR SEASONS

FLOWER	Winter	Spring	Summer	Fall
Allium		X	X	
Alstroemeria	X	X	X	X
Amaryllis	X		X	
Anemone	X	X		X
Aster	X	X	X	X
Baby's Breath	X	X	X	X
Bachelor's Button	X	X	X	X
Billy Buttons		X	X	
Bird of Paradise	X	X	X	X
Bouvardia	X	X	X	X
Calla Lily	X	X	X	X
Carnation	X	X	X	X
Celosia		X	X	
Chrysanthemum	X	X	X	X
Daffodils		X		
Dahlia			X	X
Delphinium			X	X
Eucalyptus	X	X	X	X
Freesia	X	X	X	X
Gardenia	X	X	X	X
Gerbera	X	X	X	X
Gladiolus	X	X	X	X
Iris	X	X	X	X
Liatris	X	X	X	X
Lily	X	X	X	X

FLOWER	Winter	Spring	Summer	Fall
Lily of the Valley		X		
Lisianthus		X	X	X
Narcissus	X	X		X
Nerine	X	X	X	X
Orchid (Cattleya)	X	X	X	X
Orchid (Cymbidium)	X	X	X	X
Peony		X		
Pincushion			X	
Protea	X			X
Queen Anne's Lace			X	
Ranunculus		X		
Rose	X	X	X	X
Saponaria			X	
Snapdragon		X	X	X
Speedwell			X	
Star of Bethlehem	X			X
Statice	X	X	X	X
Stephanotis	X	X	X	X
Stock	X	X	X	X
Sunflower		X	X	X
Sweet Pea		X		
Tuberose			X	X
Tulip	X	X		
Waxflower	X	X		

NOTES

DECORATIONS

DECORATIONS CAN ENHANCE YOUR WEDDING by unifying every component of your ceremony and reception. Decorations include anything from floral arrangements, twinkling lights, and centerpieces to more personal touches, such as seating cards, menus, favors, and more. Most items, such as stationery and place settings, are purchased or arranged based on a unified theme. For example, if the theme is Asian inspired, paper lanterns and take-out boxes can create a unique ambience with a theme-specific flair.

DETAILED DECORATIONS

When guests enter your reception, they should make their way to your guest book, and then to find their seating card.

Options: The traditional guest book is an album of blank pages or photos of the couple with space around the edges for guests to write their names and a thoughtful message.

A modern twist on the guest book is a wishing tree. Provide a small potted tree and a basket of small cards with a loop of ribbon or string. Guests write loving wishes on the cards and hang them on the tree. The bride and groom keep the wishes and plant the tree wherever they would like to have a special reminder of their wedding day.

Seating cards are designed to tell guests where they will be seated at the reception. A simple card with calligraphy is beautiful and classic, but there are many creative options. For instance, choose a nature-friendly option and use a pressed tree leaf with each guest's name and table number on it.

Things to Consider: Keep in mind that your guest book should have enough room for everyone in attendance to write a personal message to you if they wish.

Seating cards are an aspect of planning that can wait until the end, once the guest list has been confirmed.

Price Range: $1 - $2 each

TABLE CENTERPIECES

Table centerpieces lend style and elegance to your reception. Each of the tables at your reception, including the head table, should be decorated with a centerpiece.

DECORATIONS

Options: Flowers are, of course, a popular choice for table centerpieces. Floral centerpieces should mimic the color scheme and floral theme for the entire wedding. For contemporary weddings, trends include low table arrangements with large statement flowers, such as protea and chrysanthemum, or grouping multiple small vases together as a centerpiece. Calla lilies or long-stemmed blooms are also perfect for more contemporary ceremonies.

To invoke a classic bit of symbolism place blue and white irises at the bride and groom's table to signify that marriage will have both vibrant and pale times.

Another beautiful trend is using non-floral elements like feathers, fruit, pods, pepper berries, shells, lace, and stones in centerpieces. Something as simple as filling a vase with lemons or green apples adds a vibrant touch to a table. An arrangement of shells makes a very nice centerpiece for a seaside reception.

Candles and mirrors also create an intimate atmosphere. Votive candles set on top of a mirror make a romantic centerpiece for an evening reception. Another elegant trend is floating candles in low-lying vases of water.

Naturally, the options are endless. This is the perfect opportunity to get creative!

Things to Consider: The centerpiece for the head table should be larger or more elaborate than the ones for the other tables. Make sure that centerpieces are kept low or narrow enough so as not to hinder conversation among guests seated across from each other.

Consider using a centerpiece that your guests can take home as a memento of your wedding. Or donate leftover centerpieces to retirement homes as a means of recycling while spreading the joy and beauty of your wedding day.

Tips to Save Money: Make your own table centerpieces using inexpensive materials like fruit or stones. Non-floral items will always make for a less-expensive option. Or transport floral arrangements from the ceremony site at your reception and reuse them.

Finally, if you hold your wedding around the time of a major holiday, many venues with have holiday decorations available that you may want to use, such as pinecone centerpieces or greenery.

Price Range: $10 - $100 each

TYPE OF DECORATION	Description	Website/Company	Quantity	Price
Themed Decorations				
Guest Book				
Seating Cards				
Table Numbers				
Head Table Centerpiece				
Guest Tables' Centerpieces				
Other:				
Other:				
Other:				

NOTES

TRANSPORTATION & RENTALS

✿ ✿ ✿

Karen French

KAREN FRENCH

KAREN FRENCH

KAREN FRENCH

KAREN FRENCH

KAREN FRENCH

TRANSPORTATION

IT IS CUSTOMARY FOR THE BRIDE AND HER FATHER TO RIDE TO THE CEREMONY site together on the wedding day. You may also include some or all members of your wedding party. Normally a procession to the church begins with the bride's mother and several of the bride's attendants in the first vehicle. If desired, you can provide a second vehicle for the rest of the attendants. The bride and her father will go in the last vehicle. This vehicle will also be used to transport the bride and groom to the reception site after the ceremony.

TRANSPORTATION

Options: There are various options for transportation. The most popular choice is a limousine since it is large and open, and can accommodate several people, as well as your bridal gown. You can also choose to rent a car that symbolizes your personality as a couple.

There are luxury cars such as Mercedes Benz, sports cars such as a Ferraris, and vintage vehicles such as 1950s Thunderbirds or 1930s Cadillacs. If your ceremony and reception sites are fairly close together, and if weather permits, you might want to consider a more romantic form of transportation, such as a horse-drawn carriage.

Things to Consider: In some areas of the country, limousines are booked on a three-hour minimum basis.

Beware: Make sure the company you choose is fully licensed and has liability insurance. Do not pay the full amount until after the event.

Tips to Save Money: Consider hiring only one large limousine. This limousine can transport you, your parents, and your attendants to the ceremony, and then you and your new husband from the ceremony to the reception.

Price Range: $35 - $100 per hour

TRANSPORTATION COMPARISON CHART

QUESTIONS	POSSIBILITY 1	POSSIBILITY 2
What is the name of the transportation service?		
What is the website and email of the transportation service?		
What is the address of the transportation service?		
What is the name and phone number of my contact person?		
How many years have you been in business?		
How many vehicles do you have available?		
Can you provide a backup vehicle in case of an emergency?		
What types of vehicles are available?		
What are the various sizes of vehicles available?		
How old are the vehicles?		
How many drivers are available?		
Can you guarantee which drivers will be provided and tell me more about their experience?		
How do your drivers dress for weddings?		
Do you have liability insurance?		
What is the minimum amount of time required to rent a vehicle?		
What is the cost per hour? Two hours? Three hours?		
How much gratuity is expected?		
What is your payment/cancellation policy?		

POSSIBILITY 3	POSSIBILITY 4	POSSIBILITY 5	POSSIBILITY 6

WEDDING DAY TRANSPORTATION CHART

TO CEREMONY SITE

NAME	Pickup Time	Pickup Location	Vehicle/Driver
Bride			
Groom			
Bride's Parents			
Groom's Parents			
Bridesmaids			
Ushers			
Other:			
Other:			
Other:			

TO RECEPTION SITE

NAME	Pickup Time	Pickup Location	Vehicle/Driver
Bride and Groom			
Bride's Parents			
Groom's Parents			
Bridesmaids			
Ushers			
Other:			
Other:			

RENTAL ITEMS

NOT ALL ITEMS NEED TO BE PURCHASED FOR THE ceremony and reception. There are many items that you have the option of renting, such as the tent, canopy, chairs, and linens for the reception. This allows you to host a reception in your own home or in less traditional locations, such as an art museum, a local park, or at the beach. Be sure to take into account the cost of all these rental items when creating your budget.

BRIDAL SLIP

The bridal slip is an undergarment which gives the bridal gown its proper shape.

Things to Consider: Be sure to wear the same slip you'll be wearing on your wedding day during your fittings. Many bridal salons rent slips. Schedule an appointment to pick up your slip one week before the wedding; otherwise, you run the risk of not having one available on your wedding day. If rented, the slip will have to be returned shortly after the wedding. Arrange for someone to do this for you within the allotted time.

Tips to Save Money: Rent a slip rather than purchasing one; chances are, you will never use it again.

Price Range: $25 - $75

CEREMONY ACCESSORIES

Ceremony rental accessories are the additional items needed for the ceremony that are not included in the ceremony site fee.

Options: Ceremony rental accessories may include the following items:

Aisle Runner: A thin rug made of plastic, paper or cloth extending the length of the aisle. It is rolled out after the mothers are seated, right before the processional. Plastic or paper doesn't work well on grass; but if you must use one of these types of runners, make sure the grass is clipped short.

Kneeling Cushion: A small cushion or pillow placed in front of the altar where the bride and groom kneel for their wedding blessing.

RENTAL ITEMS

Arch (Christian): A white lattice or brass arch where the bride and groom exchange their vows, often decorated with flowers and greenery.

Chuppah (Jewish): A canopy under which a Jewish ceremony is performed, symbolizing cohabitation and consummation.

You may also need to consider renting audio equipment, aisle stanchions, candelabra, candles, candle-lighters, chairs, heaters, a gift table, a guest book stand, and a canopy.

Things to Consider: If you plan to rent any accessories for your ceremony, make sure the rental supplier has been in business for a reasonable period of time, and has a good reputation. Reserve the items you need well in advance. Find out the company's payment, reservation, and cancellation policies.

Some companies allow you to reserve emergency items, such as heaters or canopies, without having to pay for them unless needed. In that case, you would need to call the rental company a day or two in advance to request the items. If someone else requests the items you have reserved, the company should give you the right of first refusal.

Tips to Save Money: When considering a ceremony outside of a church, figure out the cost of rental items. Negotiate a package deal, if possible, by renting items for both the ceremony and the reception from the same supplier. Consider renting these items from your florist so you only have to pay one delivery fee.

Price Range: $100 - $500

TENT/CANOPY

A large tent or canopy may be required for receptions held outdoors to protect you and your guests from the sun or rain. Usually rented through party rental suppliers, tents and canopies can be expensive due to the labor involved in delivery and setting up.

Options: Tents and canopies come in different sizes and colors. Depending on the shape of your reception area, you may need to rent several smaller canopies rather than one large one. Contact several party rental suppliers to discuss the options.

Things to Consider: Consider this cost when making a decision between an outdoor and an indoor reception. In cooler weather, heaters may also be necessary if you go the outdoor route.

Tips to Save Money: Shop early and compare prices with several party rental suppliers.

Price Range: $300 - $5,000

DANCE FLOOR

A dance floor will be provided by most hotels and clubs. However, if your reception site does not have a dance floor, you may need to rent one through your caterer or a party rental supplier.

Things to Consider: When comparing prices of dance floors, include the delivery and setup fees.

Price Range: $100 - $600

TABLES/CHAIRS

You will have to provide tables and chairs for your guests if your reception site or caterer doesn't provide them as part of their package. For a full meal, you will obviously have to provide tables and seating for all guests. For a cocktail reception, you only need to provide tables and chairs for approximately 30 to 50 percent of your guests. Ask your caterer or reception site manager for advice.

Options: There are various types of tables and chairs to choose from. The most commonly used chairs for wedding receptions are typically white wooden or plastic chairs. The most common tables for receptions are round tables that seat eight guests. Often, the head table arrangement is several rectangular tables placed end-to-end to seat your entire wedding party on one side, facing your guests. Contact various party rental suppliers to find out what types of chairs and tables they carry, as well as their price ranges.

Things to Consider: When comparing prices of renting tables and chairs, include the cost of delivery and setting up.

Tips to Save Money: Attempt to negotiate free delivery and setup with party rental suppliers in exchange for giving them your business.

Price Range: $3 - $10 per person

LINEN/TABLEWARE

You will also need to provide linens and tableware for your reception if your site or caterer does not provide them as part of their package.

Options: For a sit-down reception where the meal is served by waiters and waitresses, tables are usually set with a tablecloth (often white, but may be color coordinated with the wedding), a centerpiece, and complete place settings. At a less formal buffet reception where guests serve themselves, tables are covered with a tablecloth, but place settings are not mandatory. The necessary plates and silverware may be located at the buffet table next to the food.

RENTAL ITEMS

Things to Consider: Linens and tableware depend on the formality of your reception. When comparing prices of linens and tableware, include the cost of delivery and setup.

Price Range: $3 - $25 per person

HEATERS

You may need to rent heaters if your ceremony or reception will be held outdoors. You definitely want to invest in some if the temperature could drop below 65 degrees.

Options: There are electric and gas heaters, both of which come in different sizes. Gas heaters are more popular since they do not have unsightly and unsafe electric cords.

Price Range: $25 - $75

LANTERNS

Lanterns are often used at evening receptions.

Options: Many choices are available, from fire lanterns to electric varieties, in a plethora of colors.

Things to Consider: Consider the formality of the reception and choose the proper lighting to complement your decorations.

Price Range: $6 - $60

OTHER RENTAL ITEMS (TRASH CANS, GIFT TABLE, ETC.)

If your reception site or caterer doesn't provide them, you will need to purchase, rent, or borrow other miscellaneous items for your reception, such as a gift table, trash cans, trash bags, and so on.

CEREMONY EQUIPMENT CHECKLIST

RENTAL SUPPLIER: _____   Contact Person: _____

Website: _____

Email: _____

Address: _____

City: _____   State: _____   Zip Code: _____

Phone Number: _____   Hours: _____

Payment Policy: _____

Cancellation Policy: _____

Delivery Time: _____   Tear Down Time: _____

Setup Time: _____   Pickup Time: _____

QTY.	ITEM	Description	Price	Total
	Arch/Altar		$	$
	Canopy (Chuppah)		$	$
	Backdrops		$	$
	Floor Candelabra		$	$
	Candles		$	$
	Candle Lighters		$	$
	Kneeling Bench		$	$
	Aisle Stanchions		$	$
	Aisle Runners		$	$
	Guest Book Stand		$	$
	Gift Table		$	$
	Chairs		$	$
	Audio Equipment		$	$
	Lighting		$	$
	Heating/Cooling		$	$
	Umbrellas/Tents		$	$
	Bug Eliminator		$	$
	Coat/Hat Rack		$	$
	Garbage Cans		$	$

RENTAL SUPPLIER COMPARISON CHART

QUESTIONS	POSSIBILITY 1	POSSIBILITY 2
What is the name of the party rental supplier?		
What is the address of the party rental supplier?		
What is the website and email of the party rental supplier?		
What is the name and phone number of my contact person?		
How many years have you been in business?		
What are your hours of operation?		
Do you have liability insurance?		
What is the cost per item needed?		
What is the cost of pickup and delivery?		
What is the cost of setting up the items rented?		
When would the items be delivered?		
When would the items be picked up after the event?		
What is your payment policy?		
What is your cancellation policy?		

POSSIBILITY 3	POSSIBILITY 4	POSSIBILITY 5	POSSIBILITY 6

RECEPTION EQUIPMENT CHECKLIST

RENTAL SUPPLIER: _____   Contact Person: _____

Website: _____

Email: _____

Address: _____

City: _____   State: _____   Zip Code: _____

Phone Number: _____   Hours: _____

Payment Policy: _____

Cancellation Policy: _____

Delivery Time: _____   Tear Down Time: _____

Setup Time: _____   Pickup Time: _____

QTY.	ITEM	Description	Price	Total
	Audio Equipment		$	$
	Cake Table		$	$
	Candelabras/Candles		$	$
	Canopies		$	$
	Coat/Hat Rack		$	$
	Dance Floor		$	$
	Bug Eliminator		$	$
	Garbage Cans		$	$
	Gift Table		$	$
	Guest Tables		$	$
	Heating/Cooling		$	$
	High/Booster Chairs		$	$
	Lighting		$	$
	Mirror Disco Ball		$	$
	Place Card Table		$	$
	Tents		$	$
	Umbrellas		$	$
	Visual Equipment		$	$
	Wheelchair Ramp		$	$

GIFTS & PARTIES

Karen French

GIFTS

GIFTS ARE A WONDERFUL WAY TO SHOW YOUR APPRECIATION to family, friends, members of your wedding party, as well as all the other folks who have assisted you in your wedding planning process. Couples usually like to exchange something meaningful on their wedding day as well.

BRIDE'S GIFT

The bride's gift is typically personal, such as a piece of jewelry.

Options: A string of pearls, watch, pearl earrings, jewelry box, perfume, or lingerie.

Things to Consider: This gift should be given only if your budget allows.

Tips to Save Money: A heartfelt card from the groom proclaiming his love for the bride is a very special, yet inexpensive gift. If you are writing your own vows, the groom can opt to print and frame his vows for a touching and cost-effective gift.

Price Range: $50 - $1,000

GROOM'S GIFT

The groom's gift is traditionally given by the bride to the groom.

Options: A watch, photo of the bride framed in silver or crystal, album of boudoir photos, golf clubs, rare wine or liquor, or electronics.

Things to Consider: This gift should be given only if your budget allows.

Tips to Save Money: If you are writing original vows, a great, cost-effective option is to have the bride's vows to the groom framed. A loving card or letter from the bride is also just as meaningful as a gift, and is inexpensive.

Price Range: $50 - $1,000

BRIDESMAIDS' GIFTS

Bridesmaids' gifts are given by the bride to her bridesmaids and maid of honor as a permanent keepsake of the wedding. Traditional gifts are those that can be used both during and after the wedding, such as jewelry.

Options: Jewelry, hairpieces, pashminas or wraps, personalized sweat suits or tank tops, favorite beauty products, certificates for a spa treatment before the wedding day, tote or cosmetics bags, jewelry boxes, or customized stationery.

Things to Consider: Bridesmaids' gifts are usually presented at the bridesmaids' luncheon, if there is one, or at the rehearsal dinner. The gift to the maid of honor may be similar to the bridesmaids' gifts, but should be a bit more expensive.

Tips to Save Money: A beautiful photo album from the wedding or a framed photo of the bridesmaid and her date can make a nice, cost-conscious gift.

Price Range: $25 - $200 per gift

USHERS' GIFTS

Ushers' gifts are given by the groom to his ushers as a permanent keepsake of the wedding.

Options: Wallet or money clip, cigars, knives, flask, sporting equipment, luxury shaving kit, or rare wine or liquor.

Things to Consider: The groom should deliver his gifts to the ushers at the bachelor party or at the rehearsal dinner. The gift to the best man may be similar to the others' gifts, but should be a bit more expensive.

Tips to Save Money: Have an inexpensive keepsake item engraved with your ushers' initials and their wedding dates. For instance, an engraved flask can cost less than $30 per gift.

Price Range: $25 - $200 per gift

RECIPIENT	Gift	Website/Company

NOTES

PARTIES

WEDDINGS ARE OFTEN MUCH MORE THAN A ONE-DAY CELEBRATION. There can be plenty of festivities before and after the actual wedding day. An engagement party, bridal shower, bachelor party, bachelorette party, bridesmaids' luncheon, rehearsal dinner, and day-after brunch are traditional events.

ENGAGEMENT PARTY

The engagement party is generally thrown by the bride's family to celebrate the big news. Gifts are not required at this party.

Things to Consider: If your schedule won't allow for it, an engagement party is by no means a requirement.

Options: An engagement party is typically held in your parents' home; however, renting a space or having dinner at a restaurant are also popular options.

BRIDAL SHOWER

Traditionally, your bridal shower is thrown by your maid of honor and bridesmaids, unless they are members of your immediate family. Because a shower is a gift-giving occasion, it is not considered socially acceptable for anyone in your immediate family to host this event. If your mother or sisters wish to be involved, have them offer to help with the cost of the event or offer their home for

it. The agenda usually includes some games and gift-opening. Be sure to have someone keep track of which gift is from whom.

Things to Consider: You may have several showers thrown for you. When creating your guest lists, be sure not to invite the same people to multiple showers (the exception being members of the wedding party, who may be invited to all showers without the obligation of bringing a gift). Only include people who have been invited to the wedding—the only exception to this is a work shower, to which all coworkers may be invited, whether or not they are attending the wedding.

Options: Tea parties, spa days, cocktail parties, and traditional at-home events are all festive choices—these days even men are invited, as coed showers become more and more popular! Generally, the event is themed (lingerie, cooking, home décor), and the invitation should give guests an idea of what type of gift to bring.

PARTIES

BACHELOR PARTY

The bachelor party is a male-only affair typically organized by the best man. He is responsible for selecting the date and reserving the place and entertainment, as well as inviting the groom's male friends and family. Your best man should also assign responsibilities to the ushers, as they should help with the organization of this party.

Things to Consider: Your best man should not plan your bachelor party for the night before the wedding, since chances are that you will consume a fair amount of alcohol and stay up late. You don't want to have a hangover or be exhausted during your wedding. It is much more appropriate to have the bachelor party two or three nights before the wedding.

Your best man should designate a driver for you and for those who will be drinking alcohol. Remember, you and your best man are responsible for the well-being of everybody invited to the party.

Options: A bachelor party doesn't have to be the wild, debaucherous affair everyone imagines. Great options include dinner and drinks, golf, a casino trip, sporting event, brewery tour, skydiving, or camping.

BACHELORETTE PARTY

The bachelorette party is organized by the maid of honor and is a chance for the bridesmaids and female family members to celebrate together.

Things to Consider: Do not plan your bachelorette party for the night before the wedding or you risk being tired and hung over at your event. Plan to have this party a few days before the wedding or in the months leading up to it.

Options: Male strippers do not have to be a part of a fun bachelorette party! You might enjoy dinner and drinks, a spa day, wine tasting, a yoga or Pilates retreat, or even a themed a scavenger hunt.

BRIDESMAIDS' LUNCHEON

The bridesmaids' luncheon is given by the bride for her bridesmaids. It is not a shower; rather, it is simply a time for good friends to get together formally before the bride changes her status from single to married.

Things to Consider: You can give your bridesmaids their gifts at this gathering. Otherwise, plan to give them their gifts at the rehearsal dinner.

Price Range: $12 - $60 per person

REHEARSAL DINNER

It is customary that the groom's parents host a dinner party following the rehearsal, the evening before the wedding. The dinner usually includes the bridal party, their spouses or guests, both sets of parents, close family members, some out-of-town guests, the officiant, and the wedding consultant and/or coordinator.

Options: The rehearsal dinner party can be held just about anywhere, from a restaurant, hotel, or private hall to the groom's parents' home.

Tips to Save Money: Restaurants specializing in Mexican food or pizza are fun yet inexpensive options. The rehearsal dinner doesn't have to be a fancy event.

Price Range: $10 - $100 per person

DAY-AFTER BRUNCH

Many times the newlyweds will want to host a brunch the day after the wedding to spend one last bit of time with their guests and to thank them for coming to the wedding. This is especially true if many guests came from out of town, or if you are having a destination wedding.

Things to Consider: Brunch can be much less formal than the rest of the wedding. Ask your family to help create this casual get-together by cooking or picking up brunch food items.

Choose a reasonable time for the brunch: Not too early, as many guests will be recovering from the festivities of the reception, but not too late, as out-of-town guests will have travel arrangements to attend to.

Tips to Save Money: Keep the brunch menu simple—have bagels, croissants, jams, fruit, coffee, and juice. If many guests are staying at the same hotel, ask the hotel if you can have the brunch in their breakfast room.

Price Range: $5 - $25 per person

PARTIES CHART

PARTY	Location	Date	Time	Notes
Engagement Party				
Bridal Shower				
Bachelor Party				
Bachelorette Party				
Bridesmaids' Luncheon				
Rehearsal Dinner				
Day-After Brunch				
Other:				
Other:				

Things to Know

Karen French

LEGAL MATTERS

WITH ALL THAT IS INVOLVED IN PLANNING A WEDDING, it is easy to forget some simple but necessary legal matters. Be sure that you don't forget to consider or complete the following items.

MARRIAGE LICENSE

Marriage license requirements are state-regulated, and may be obtained from the County Clerk in most county courthouses.

Options: Some states (California and Nevada, for example) offer two types of marriage licenses: a public license and a confidential one. The public license is the most common one, and it requires that at least one witness be present at your ceremony and sign the license. It can only be obtained at the County Clerk's Office.

The confidential license, on the other hand, will not go on public record, and can usually be obtained from most Justices of the Peace. An oath must be taken in order to receive either license.

Things to Consider: Requirements vary from state to state, but generally include the following points:

1. Applying for and paying the fee for the marriage license. There is usually a waiting period before the license is valid, and a lim-ited time before it expires.

2. Meeting residency requirements for the state and/or county where the ceremony will take place.

3. Meeting the legal age requirements for both bride and groom, or having parental consent.

4. Presenting any required identification, i.e. birth or baptismal certificates, marriage eligibility, or other documents.

Price Range: $20 - $100

PRENUPTIAL AGREEMENT

A prenuptial agreement is a legal contract between the bride and groom itemizing the property each brings into the marriage, and explaining how those properties will be divided in case of divorce or death. Although you can write your own agreement, it is advisable to have an attorney draw up or review the document. The two of you should be represented by different attorneys.

Things to Consider: Consider a prenuptial agreement if one or both of you have a significant amount of capital or assets, or if there are children involved from a previous marriage. If you are going to live in a different state after the wedding, consider having an attorney from that state draw up or review your document.

Nobody likes to talk about divorce or death when planning a wedding, but it is very important to give these issues your utmost consideration. By drawing a prenuptial agreement, you encourage open communication, and get a better idea of each other's needs and expectations. You should also consider drawing up or reviewing your wills at this time.

Tips to Save Money: Some software packages allow you to write your own will and prenuptial agreement, which can save you substantial attorney's fees. However, if you decide to draw either agreement on your own, you should still have an attorney review it.

Price Range: $500 - $3,000

TAXES

Don't forget to figure in the cost of taxes on all the taxable items you purchase for your wedding. Many people make a big mistake by not figuring out the taxes they will have to pay for their wedding expenses. For example, if you are planning a reception for 250 guests with an estimated cost of $60 per person for food and beverages, your pretax expenses would be $15,000. A sales tax of 7.5 percent would mean an additional expense of $1,125! Find out what the sales tax is in your area, and which items are taxable and figure this expense into your overall budget.

NAME & ADDRESS CHANGE FORM

TO WHOM IT MAY CONCERN:

This is to inform you of my recent marriage, and to request a change of name and/or address. The following information will be effective as of: _____

My account/policy number is: _____

Under the name of: _____

PREVIOUS INFORMATION:

Husband's Name: _____ Phone Number: _____

Previous Address: _____

Wife's Maiden Name: _____ Phone Number: _____

Previous Address: _____

NEW INFORMATION:

Husband's Name: _____ Phone Number: _____

Wife's Name: _____ Phone Number: _____

New Address: _____

SPECIAL INSTRUCTIONS:

- ❏ Change name
- ❏ Change address/phone
- ❏ Add spouse's name
- ❏ Send necessary forms to include my spouse on my policy/account
- ❏ We plan to continue service
- ❏ We plan to discontinue service after: _____

If you have any questions, please feel free to contact us at: ( ) _____

Husband's Signature: _____

Wife's Signature: _____

CHANGE OF ADDRESS WORKSHEET

COMPANY	Account or Policy No.	Phone or Address	Done ✔
Auto Insurance			
Auto Registration			
Bank Accounts			
1)			
2)			
3)			
Credit Cards			
1)			
2)			
3)			
4)			
Dentists			
Doctors			
Driver's License			
Employee Records			
Insurance: Dental			
Insurance: Disability			
Insurance: Homeowner's			
Insurance: Life			
Insurance: Renter's			
Insurance: Other			
IRA Accounts			
1)			
2)			
3)			
Leases			
1)			
2)			
Loan Companies			
1)			
2)			
3)			

COMPANY	Account or Policy No.	Phone or Address	Done ✔
Magazines			
Memberships			
1)			
2)			
3)			
Mortgage			
Newspapers			
1)			
2)			
Passport			
Pensions			
Post Office			
Property Title			
Retirement Accounts			
1)			
2)			
Safe Deposit Box			
School Records			
1)			
2)			
3)			
Social Security			
Stockbroker			
Taxes			
Telephone Company			
Utilities			
Voter Registration			
Will/Trust			
Other:			
Other:			
Other:			
Other:			

NOTES

WHO PAYS FOR WHAT

BRIDE AND/OR BRIDE'S FAMILY

- Engagement party
- Wedding consultant's fee
- Bridal gown, veil, and accessories
- Wedding stationery, calligraphy, and postage
- Wedding gift for bridal couple
- Groom's wedding ring
- Gifts for bridesmaids
- Bridesmaids' bouquets
- Pre-wedding parties and bridesmaids' luncheon
- Photography and videography
- Wedding guest book and other accessories
- Total cost of the ceremony, including location, flowers, music, rental items, and accessories
- Total cost of the reception, including location, flowers, music, rental items, accessories, food, beverages, cake, decorations, favors, etc.
- Transportation for bridal party to ceremony and reception
- Own attire and travel expenses

GROOM AND/OR GROOM'S FAMILY

- Own travel expenses and attire
- Rehearsal dinner
- Wedding gift for bridal couple
- Bride's wedding ring
- Gifts for groom's attendants
- Bride's bouquet and going away corsage
- Mothers' and grandmothers' corsages
- All boutonnieres
- Officiant's fee
- Marriage license
- Honeymoon expenses

WHO PAYS FOR WHAT

ATTENDANTS

- Own attire except flowers
- Travel expenses
- Bridal shower paid for by maid of honor and bridesmaids
- Bachelor party paid for by best man and ushers
- Bachelorette party paid for by maid of honor and bridesmaids

WEDDING
FORMATIONS

THE FOLLOWING SECTION ILLUSTRATES THE TYPICAL CEREMONY FORMATIONS (processional, recessional, and altar lineup) for both Christian and Jewish weddings, as well as the typical formations for the receiving line, head table, and parents' tables at the reception.

These ceremony formations are included in the *Wedding Party Responsibility Cards*, published by WS Publishing Group. This attractive set of cards makes it very easy for members of your wedding party to remember their place in these formations. Give one card to each member of your wedding party—they will appreciate it. This book of cards is available at most major bookstores.

$\mathscr{A}$LTAR $\mathscr{L}$INE $\mathscr{U}$P

Bride's Pews   Groom's Pews

ABBREVIATIONS

B=Bride	GF=Groom's Father	G=Groom	GM=Groom's Mother
BM=Best Man	BMa=Bridesmaids	MH=Maid of Honor	U=Ushers
BF=Bride's Father	FG=Flower Girl	BMo=Bride's Mother	RB=Ring Bearer
O=Officiant			

Processional

Recessional

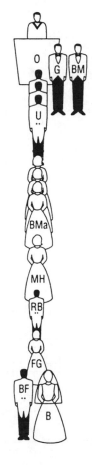
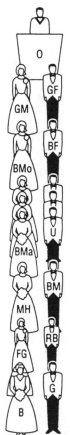

ABBREVIATIONS

B=Bride

BM=Best Man

BF=Bride's Father

O=Officiant

GF=Groom's Father

BMa=Bridesmaids

FG=Flower Girl

G=Groom

MH=Maid of Honor

BMo=Bride's Mother

GM=Groom's Mother

U=Ushers

RB=Ring Bearer

*A*LTAR *L*INE *U*P

Groom's Pews   Bride's Pews

ABBREVIATIONS

B=Bride	GF=Groom's Father	G=Groom	GM=Groom's Mother
BM=Best Man	BMa=Bridesmaids	MH=Maid of Honor	U=Ushers
BF=Bride's Father	FG=Flower Girl	BMo=Bride's Mother	RB=Ring Bearer
R=Rabbi			

*P*ROCESSIONAL

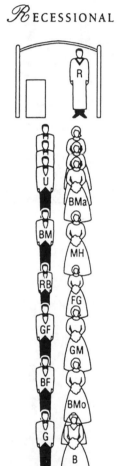

*R*ECESSIONAL

ABBREVIATIONS

B=Bride	GF=Groom's Father	G=Groom	GM=Groom's Mother
BM=Best Man	BMa=Bridesmaids	MH=Maid of Honor	U=Ushers
BF=Bride's Father	FG=Flower Girl	BMo=Bride's Mother	RB=Ring Bearer
R=Rabbi			

ℛECEIVING ℒINE

ℋEAD ℐABLE

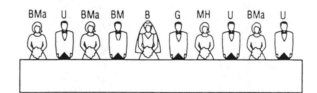

𝒫ARENTS' ℐABLE

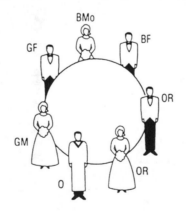

ABBREVIATIONS

B=Bride	GF=Groom's Father	G=Groom	GM=Groom's Mother
BM=Best Man	BMa=Bridesmaids	MH=Maid of Honor	U=Ushers
BF=Bride's Father	OR=Other Relatives	BMo=Bride's Mother	O=Officiant

THINGS TO BRING

TO THE REHEARSAL

BRIDE'S LIST

- ❑ Wedding announcements (give to maid of honor to mail after wedding)
- ❑ Bridesmaids' gifts (if not already given)
- ❑ Camera, memory card, battery, charger, etc.
- ❑ Fake bouquet or ribbon bouquet from bridal shower
- ❑ Groom's gift (if not already given)
- ❑ Reception maps and wedding programs
- ❑ Rehearsal information and ceremony formations
- ❑ Flower girl basket and ring bearer pillow
- ❑ Seating diagrams for head table and parents' tables
- ❑ Wedding schedule of events/timeline
- ❑ CD/MP3 player with wedding music

GROOM'S LIST

- ❑ Bride's gift (if not already given)
- ❑ Marriage license
- ❑ Ushers' gifts (if not already given)
- ❑ Service providers' fees to give to best man or wedding consultant so he or she can pay them at the wedding

THINGS TO BRING

TO THE CEREMONY

BRIDE'S LIST
- ❏ Aspirin/Antacid
- ❏ Bobby pins
- ❏ Breath spray/mints
- ❏ Bridal gown
- ❏ Bridal gown box
- ❏ Cake knife
- ❏ Going away clothes
- ❏ Clear nail polish
- ❏ Deodorant
- ❏ Garter
- ❏ Gloves
- ❏ Groom's ring
- ❏ Guest book
- ❏ Hairbrush
- ❏ Hair spray

- ❏ Headpiece
- ❏ Iron
- ❏ Jewelry
- ❏ Lint brush
- ❏ Luggage
- ❏ Makeup
- ❏ Mirror
- ❏ Nail polish
- ❏ Panty hose
- ❏ Passport
- ❏ Perfume
- ❏ Personal camera
- ❏ Plume pen for guest book
- ❏ Powder
- ❏ Purse

- ❏ Safety pins
- ❏ Scotch tape/masking tape
- ❏ Sewing kit
- ❏ Shoes
- ❏ Something old
- ❏ Something new
- ❏ Something borrowed
- ❏ Something blue
- ❏ Sixpence (shiny penny) for shoe
- ❏ Spot remover
- ❏ Straight pins
- ❏ Tampons or feminine napkins
- ❏ Tissues
- ❏ Toasting goblets
- ❏ Toothbrush and paste

GROOM'S LIST
- ❏ Airline tickets
- ❏ Announcements
- ❏ Aspirin/Antacid
- ❏ Breath spray/mints
- ❏ Bride's ring
- ❏ Going away clothes
- ❏ Cologne
- ❏ Cuff links

- ❏ Cummerbund
- ❏ Deodorant
- ❏ Hair comb
- ❏ Hair product
- ❏ Lint brush
- ❏ Luggage
- ❏ Necktie
- ❏ Passport

- ❏ Shirt
- ❏ Shoes
- ❏ Socks
- ❏ Tissues
- ❏ Toothbrush and paste
- ❏ Tuxedo
- ❏ Underwear

Calendar & Timelines

❀ ❀ ❀

Karen French

KAREN FRENCH

KAREN FRENCH

KAREN FRENCH

KAREN FRENCH

KAREN FRENCH

WEDDING PLANNING CALENDAR

THE NEXT SEVERAL MONTHS WILL BE FILLED WITH IMPORTANT DATES AND TASKS. Make sure you allow yourself adequate time to book your ceremony and reception site in advance, create seating arrangements, schedule meetings with caters, photographers, florists, and bakeries—and still have time to take care of any other wedding planning details.

Use the 9-month calendar on the following pages to document your wedding date, parties, all of your appointments, scheduled payments, and any other items you want to complete by a certain date.

If you are planning on a health, fitness, and/or beauty regime during your wedding planning process, write down your routine on this calendar as well to keep you on track and help you reach your goals.

To use this calendar, assign the last calendar page provided for the month your wedding will take place. Then, work backwards and simply fill in the month, year, and number of months before your wedding at the top of each page. Next, fill in the dates based on each month.

WEDDING PLANNING CALENDAR

Month:_____ 20_____ Number of months before wedding: _____

Sunday	Monday	Tuesday	Wednesday	Thursday	Friday	Saturday

Notes:_____

_____

Month:_____ 20_____ Number of months before wedding: _____

Sunday	Monday	Tuesday	Wednesday	Thursday	Friday	Saturday

Notes:_____

_____

WEDDING PLANNING CALENDAR

Month:_____ 20_____ Number of months before wedding: _____

Sunday	Monday	Tuesday	Wednesday	Thursday	Friday	Saturday

Notes:_____

_____

Month:_____ 20_____ Number of months before wedding: _____

Sunday	Monday	Tuesday	Wednesday	Thursday	Friday	Saturday

Notes:_____

WEDDING PLANNING CALENDAR

Month:_____ 20_____ Number of months before wedding: _____

Sunday	Monday	Tuesday	Wednesday	Thursday	Friday	Saturday

Notes:_____

_____

Month:_____ 20_____ Number of months before wedding: _____

Sunday	Monday	Tuesday	Wednesday	Thursday	Friday	Saturday
☐	☐	☐	☐	☐	☐	☐
☐	☐	☐	☐	☐	☐	☐
☐	☐	☐	☐	☐	☐	☐
☐	☐	☐	☐	☐	☐	☐
☐	☐	☐	☐	☐	☐	☐

Notes:_____

_____

WEDDING PLANNING CALENDAR

Month:_____ 20_____ Number of months before wedding: _____

Sunday	Monday	Tuesday	Wednesday	Thursday	Friday	Saturday

Notes:_____

_____

Month:_____ 20_____ Number of months before wedding: _____

Sunday	Monday	Tuesday	Wednesday	Thursday	Friday	Saturday

Notes:_____

_____

WEDDING PLANNING CALENDAR

Month:_____ 20_____ Number of months before wedding: _____

Sunday	Monday	Tuesday	Wednesday	Thursday	Friday	Saturday

Notes:_____

_____

TIMELINES

THE FOLLOWING SECTION INCLUDES TWO DIFFERENT TIMELINES (or schedules of events) for your wedding day: one for members of your wedding party and one for the various service providers you have hired. Use these timelines to help your wedding party and service providers understand their roles and where they need to be throughout your wedding day. This will also give you a much better idea of how your special day will unfold.

When preparing your timeline, first, list the time that your wedding ceremony will begin. Then work forward or backwards, using the sample as your guide. The samples included give you an idea of how much time each event typically takes. Feel free to change the amount of time allotted for any event when customizing your own timeline.

WEDDING PARTY TIMELINE (SAMPLE)

This is a sample timeline.
Create your own timeline on the following page.

TIME	DESCRIPTION	BRIDE	BRIDE'S MOTHER	BRIDE'S FATHER	MAID OF HONOR	BRIDESMAIDS	BRIDE'S FAMILY	GROOM	GROOM'S MOTHER	GROOM'S FATHER	BEST MAN	USHERS	GROOM'S FAMILY	FLOWER GIRL	RING BEARER
2:00 PM	Manicurist appointment	✓	✓		✓	✓									
2:30 PM	Hair/makeup appointment	✓	✓		✓	✓									
4:15 PM	Arrive at dressing site	✓	✓		✓	✓									
4:30 PM	Arrive at dressing site							✓			✓	✓			
4:45 PM	Pre-ceremony photos							✓	✓	✓	✓	✓	✓		
5:15 PM	Arrive at ceremony site							✓	✓	✓	✓	✓	✓		
5:15 PM	Pre-ceremony photos	✓	✓	✓	✓	✓	✓								
5:20 PM	Give officiant marriage license and fees										✓				
5:20 PM	Ushers receive seating chart											✓			
5:30 PM	Ushers distribute wedding programs as guests arrive											✓			
5:30 PM	Arrive at ceremony site						✓							✓	✓
5:30 PM	Ushers direct guests to sign book											✓			
5:30 PM	Prelude music begins														
5:35 PM	Ushers begin seating guests											✓			
5:45 PM	Arrive at ceremony site	✓	✓	✓	✓	✓									
5:45 PM	Ushers seat honored guests											✓			
5:50 PM	Ushers seat groom's parents								✓	✓		✓			
5:55 PM	Ushers seat bride's mother		✓									✓			
5:55 PM	Attendants line up for procession				✓	✓	✓	✓			✓	✓		✓	✓
5:56 PM	Bride's father takes his place next to bride	✓		✓											
5:57 PM	Ushers roll out aisle runner											✓			
5:58 PM	Groom's party enters							✓			✓				
6:00 PM	Processional music begins														

This is a sample timeline.
Create your own timeline on the following page.

TIME	DESCRIPTION	BRIDE	BRIDE'S MOTHER	BRIDE'S FATHER	MAID OF HONOR	BRIDESMAIDS	BRIDE'S FAMILY	GROOM	GROOM'S MOTHER	GROOM'S FATHER	BEST MAN	USHERS	GROOM'S FAMILY	FLOWER GIRL	RING BEARER
6:00 PM	Groom's mother rises								✓						
6:01 PM	Ushers enter											✓			
6:02 PM	Wedding party marches up aisle	✓		✓	✓	✓								✓	✓
6:20 PM	Wedding party marches down aisle	✓			✓	✓		✓			✓	✓		✓	✓
6:22 PM	Parents march down aisle		✓	✓					✓	✓					
6:25 PM	Sign marriage certificate	✓			✓			✓			✓				
6:30 PM	Post-ceremony photos taken	✓	✓	✓	✓	✓	✓	✓	✓	✓	✓	✓	✓	✓	✓
6:30 PM	Cocktails and hors d'oeuvres served														
6:30 PM	Gift attendant watches gifts as guests arrive														
7:15 PM	Band/DJ announces entrance and/or receiving line forms	✓						✓							
7:45 PM	Guests are seated and dinner is served	✓	✓	✓	✓	✓	✓	✓	✓	✓	✓	✓	✓	✓	✓
8:30 PM	Toasts are given		✓	✓	✓	✓	✓		✓	✓	✓	✓	✓		
8:40 PM	First dance	✓						✓							
8:45 PM	Traditional dances	✓	✓	✓				✓	✓	✓					
9:00 PM	Open dance floor for all guests	✓	✓	✓	✓	✓	✓	✓	✓	✓	✓	✓	✓	✓	✓
9:30 PM	Bride and groom toast one another before cutting cake	✓						✓							
9:40 PM	Cake cutting ceremony	✓						✓							
10:00 PM	Bride tosses bouquet to single women	✓			✓	✓								✓	
10:10 PM	Groom removes garter from bride's leg	✓						✓							
10:15 PM	Groom tosses garter to single men							✓			✓	✓			✓
10:20 PM	Man who caught garter places it on bouquet-catching woman's leg														
10:30 PM	Distribute flower petals, rice, or birdseed to toss over couple		✓	✓	✓	✓	✓		✓	✓	✓	✓	✓	✓	✓
10:45 PM	Bride and groom make grand exit	✓						✓							

WEDDING PARTY TIMELINE (CONT'D)

Create your own timeline using this form.
Make copies and give one to each member of your wedding party.

TIME	DESCRIPTION	BRIDE	BRIDE'S MOTHER	BRIDE'S FATHER	MAID OF HONOR	BRIDESMAIDS	BRIDE'S FAMILY	GROOM	GROOM'S MOTHER	GROOM'S FATHER	BEST MAN	USHERS	GROOM'S FAMILY	FLOWER GIRL	RING BEARER

WEDDING PARTY TIMELINE (CONT'D)

Create your own timeline using this form.
Make copies and give one to each member of your wedding party.

TIME	DESCRIPTION	BRIDE	BRIDE'S MOTHER	BRIDE'S FATHER	MAID OF HONOR	BRIDESMAIDS	BRIDE'S FAMILY	GROOM	GROOM'S MOTHER	GROOM'S FATHER	BEST MAN	USHERS	GROOM'S FAMILY	FLOWER GIRL	RING BEARER

SERVICE PROVIDER TIMELINE (SAMPLE)

This is a sample timeline.
Create your own timeline on the following page.

TIME	DESCRIPTION	BAKERY	CATERER	CEREMONY MUSICIANS	OFFICIANT	OTHER	FLORIST	HAIRSTYLIST	LIMOUSINE	MAKEUP ARTIST	MANICURIST	PARTY RENTALS	PHOTOGRAPHER	RECEPTION MUSICIANS	VIDEOGRAPHER
1:00 PM	Party rental supplier delivers supplies to ceremony site											✓			
1:30 PM	Party rental supplier delivers supplies to reception site											✓			
2:00 PM	Manicurist meets bride at:										✓				
2:30 PM	Makeup artist meets bride at:									✓					
3:00 PM	Hairstylist meets bride at:							✓							
4:00 PM	Limousine picks up bridal party at:								✓						
4:15 PM	Caterer begins setting up		✓												
4:30 PM	Florist arrives at ceremony site						✓								
4:40 PM	Baker delivers cake to reception site	✓													
4:45 PM	Florist arrives at reception site						✓								
4:45 PM	Pre-ceremony photos of groom's family at:												✓		
5:00 PM	Videographer arrives at ceremony site														✓
5:15 PM	Pre-ceremony photos of bride's family at:												✓		
5:20 PM	Ceremony site decorations finalized (guest book, flowers, etc.)					✓	✓								
5:30 PM	Prelude music begins			✓											
5:45 PM	Reception site decorations finalized (gift table, place cards, flowers, etc.)		✓			✓	✓								
5:58 PM	Officiant enters				✓										
6:00 PM	Processional music begins			✓											
6:15 PM	Caterer finishes setting up		✓												
6:25 PM	Sign marriage certificate				✓								✓		✓
6:30 PM	Post-ceremony photos at:												✓		
6:30 PM	Cocktails and hors d'oeuvres served		✓												
6:30 PM	Band or DJ begins playing													✓	

This is a sample timeline.
Create your own timeline on the following page.

TIME	DESCRIPTION	BAKERY	CATERER	CEREMONY MUSICIANS	OFFICIANT	OTHER	FLORIST	HAIRSTYLIST	LIMOUSINE	MAKEUP ARTIST	MANICURIST	PARTY RENTALS	PHOTOGRAPHER	RECEPTION MUSICIANS	VIDEOGRAPHER
6:30 PM	Transport guest book and gifts to reception site					✓									
6:45 PM	Move arch/flowers to reception site					✓	✓								
7:00 PM	Limousine picks up bride and groom at ceremony site								✓						
7:15 PM	Band/DJ announces entrance of bride and groom													✓	
7:45 PM	Dinner is served		✓												
8:15 PM	Champagne served for toasts		✓												
8:30 PM	Band/DJ announces toast by best man													✓	
8:40 PM	Band/DJ announces first dance													✓	
9:00 PM	Transport gifts to:					✓									
9:30 PM	Band/DJ announces cake cutting ceremony													✓	
10:30 PM	Transport top tier of cake, cake topper, cake flowers, etc. to:					✓									
10:40 PM	Transport rental items to:					✓									
10:45 PM	Limousine picks up bride and groom at reception site								✓						
11:00 PM	Videographer departs														✓
11:00 PM	Photographer departs												✓		
11:00 PM	Wedding consultant departs					✓									
11:30 PM	Band/DJ stops playing													✓	
11:45 PM	Party rental supplier picks up supplies at ceremony/reception sites											✓			

SERVICE PROVIDER TIMELINE (CONT'D)

Create your own timeline using this form.
Make copies and give one to each of your service providers.

TIME	DESCRIPTION	BAKERY	CATERER	CEREMONY MUSICIANS	OFFICIANT	OTHER	FLORIST	HAIRSTYLIST	LIMOUSINE	MAKEUP ARTIST	MANICURIST	PARTY RENTALS	PHOTOGRAPHER	RECEPTION MUSICIANS	VIDEOGRAPHER

SERVICE PROVIDER TIMELINE (CONT'D)

Create your own timeline using this form.
Make copies and give one to each of your service providers.

TIME	DESCRIPTION	BAKERY	CATERER	CEREMONY MUSICIANS	OFFICIANT	OTHER	FLORIST	HAIRSTYLIST	LIMOUSINE	MAKEUP ARTIST	MANICURIST	PARTY RENTALS	PHOTOGRAPHER	RECEPTION MUSICIANS	VIDEOGRAPHER

NOTES

GREEN WEDDING TIPS

Karen French

KAREN FRENCH

KAREN FRENCH

KAREN FRENCH

KAREN FRENCH

KAREN FRENCH

GREEN WEDDING TIPS

THE ECO-FRIENDLY OR "GREEN" WEDDING has grown in popularity as couples look to protect the environment by choosing organic and recyclable options, as well as offsetting the negative impact their guests' travel will have on the earth. Having a green wedding makes a statement to your guests about the importance of protecting the planet from wear and tear.

Why should you consider a green wedding? According to the environmental organization Climate Care, the average wedding emits approximately 14.5 tons of carbon dioxide, one of the main gases believed to be responsible for climate change.

The average wedding involves 120 guests, each of whom must travel (either by plane, train, bus, or car) to the wedding site. Once they arrive, massive quantities of energy are used to chill their drinks and flowers, as well as and heat their hotel rooms and food. Even before the party starts, pesticides are used to grow the flowers and produce, and gifts are sent wrapped in extensive packaging and delivered by plane and truck.

More and more couples are looking for ways to offset the impact of their wedding on the environment, while still making their event beautiful and memorable. According to a survey by Condé Nast, publisher of *Brides* magazine, 60 percent of couples say it is important to consider the environment in their wedding; however, only 33 percent of couples surveyed were planning on having green weddings. This indicates that while the majority of couples care about keeping their weddings eco-friendly, most aren't sure how to do to execute it.

So how can you plan a green wedding that's still beautiful and chic? Actually, there are more options than ever! The wonderful thing about planning a green wedding is you can incorporate as many or as few green suggestions into your day as you want. You might host a small, eco-friendly group where your guests eat organic greens by soy candlelight as you don a hemp gown—but you can also stay fairly conventional by employing green twists on traditional wedding concepts. For example, you might simply serve a seasonal menu or buying locally grown flowers, even if they have been grown by traditional farming methods. How far you decide to take your green wedding is really up to you, your partner, your beliefs, and your budget.

Know that just because you decide to do a few things green doesn't mean you have to do everything that way. Feel comfortable sending invitations printed on recycled paper but splurging on a dress made from conventional fabric. Because we know that brides and grooms will want to pick and choose where they go green, the tips offered in this chapter provide a range of ideas, covering everything from small eco-friendly touches to intense green wedding overhauls.

And in the end, the simplest way to "go green" with your wedding is to have a smaller affair. Indeed, at the heart of the environmental movement is a commitment to simplification, conservation, and avoiding waste. Even if you don't buy a single organic product, you can have a green wedding if you simply reduce the amount of waste your wedding creates.

This chapter is filled with tips that will help you reflect environmentally sound principles in your wedding, while possibly cutting costs and reducing the amount of waste your big day produces. When you see how simple it is to incorporate a few green touches into your wedding, you'll see why "eco-chic" is replacing "bigger is better" when it comes to many couples' weddings!

CEREMONY

Eco-Tip #1: Let Nature Be the Site of Your Wedding

Indoor weddings require massive amounts of water, electricity, and air conditioning. Plus, they are typically plain spaces that must be brought to life with expensive and wasteful decorations. Therefore, aim to hold as much of your wedding outdoors as possible. Choose a site rich in natural beauty to minimize both your need to decorate and use a lot of energy. A garden in full-bloom reduces the need to buy flowers, for example, as does the beach of a quiet lake or a sprawling wildflower-speckled lawn.

Eco-Tip #2: Get Hitched In a Space that Maximizes Resources

If your wedding must be indoors, choose an LEED-certified building. LEED stands for "Leadership in Energy and Environmental Design," and means the space has been sustainably built, conserves water and electricity, and may even run on renewable energy. LEED-certified spaces can be found at www.usgbc.org, the website of the U.S. Green Building Council. Also, if you choose a country club with a golf course, check to see if it is Audubon certified. This kind, of course, meets standards for conserving water and preserving wildlife habitats.

Eco-Tip #3: Let the Site Speak For Itself

Where you hold your wedding can be an environmental statement all in itself. Instead of opting for a ballroom, restaurant, or hotel, hold your reception in a place of environmental significance. Rent space from an organization that is dedicated to nature conservation or environmental awareness, such as a bird sanctuary, aquarium, zoological society, museum, national or state park, organic co-op, art gallery, library, nonprofit organization, historical site, botanical garden, organic farm, or nature preserve.

Eco-Tip #4: Include a Tree-Planting Ritual

And, nature doesn't have to be delegated simply to the backdrop of your wedding; couples can showcase their mutual respect for the environment directly in the proceedings. Many contemporary brides and grooms plant a sapling during their ceremony. This sweet and understated ritual symbolizes the couple's strong roots, and their commitment to nurturing these roots so their marriage will grow strong and resilient. As an added personal touch, some couples have their parents assist in the tree planting to demonstrate their marriage growing from their family's strong foundation.

RINGS

Eco-Tip #5: Buy a Conflict-Free Diamond

In marriage, a diamond represents pure love. But in reality, many diamonds come from war-torn African nations, where they are mined by suffering workers, and sold to buy weapons or drugs. In fact, many of the diamonds displayed in the pretty, serene cases of jewelry stores were sold illegally and used to finance wars or even terrorist organizations. When you buy a diamond, make sure it is certified as conflict-free. Ask to see accompanying paperwork or a laser inscription number that tracks the diamond's path.

Eco-Tip #6: Use a Recycled Diamond

Since diamonds are forever, why not use one that has already been around the block? Buying a recycled diamond helps avoid the controversy that surrounds many of today's new diamonds. IDoNowIDont. com is an excellent place to get almost-new diamond jewelry. If you dislike the idea of wearing someone else's ring, take a diamond you already own to a professional jeweler. He or she will be able to create a custom ring that uses the diamond in a new and unique way.

Eco-Tip #7: Use Recycled Gold

Mining for gold is unsustainable, environmentally destructive, and releases toxic chemicals into both the atmosphere and groundwater. In fact, to excavate the gold needed to make just one wedding band, tons of mine waste is generated. Also, like diamonds, the gold mining industry often comes with dangerous working conditions and money laundering schemes, and profits sometimes fund war and civil unrest. Make sure the band you exchange with your partner is free of these elements by choosing to melt down already existing gold.

Eco-Tip #8: Consider a Ring That's Not Made from Diamonds or Gold

Considering the political and moral issues surrounding diamonds and gold these days, you may want to avoid using these materials entirely. As long as the jewelry you exchange with your partner means something to you, it is acceptable. Good alternatives are vintage rings made from alternate materials (check out www.greenkarat.com for interesting ideas). Or melt down an old ring that has special significance into a new ring. Finally, exchange wooden rings with your spouse. Many such rings have been carved from downed trees, and are lovely, unique, and inexpensive.

VOWS

Eco-Tip #9: Vow to Protect the Earth

If caring for the environment is a cornerstone of your connection to your spouse, it deserves mention in your wedding vows. Sample eco-friendly vows might resemble something like: "I, (Bride/Groom), take you (Groom/Bride), to be my (wife/husband), to be my partner in protecting the environment, and together inspire others to do the same. I vow to treat the earth with the same respect, love, and kindness that we do each other, from this day forward until death do us part."

GUEST BOOK

Eco-Tip #10: Twists on a Guest Book

Rather than wasting money and paper on a guest book, consider other ways to remember who attended your wedding. Have on display a large, handmade recycled paper panel that your guests can sign and you can frame. Or, get a signing platter. These plates come designed with your name and wedding date on them. Guests sign the plate, you bake it in the oven to seal the ink, and then keep the platter to use again and again. Check out www.guestbookplatters.com for different styles.

FLOWER GIRL BASKET

Eco-Tip #11: What's in Your Flower Girl's Basket?

Keep this classic tradition but put an eco-friendly twist on it. Have your flower girl toss organic flower petals, or ask your florist to provide wilted petals from a wedding that occurred the day before yours. Or skip flower petals entirely and have your flower girl toss unconventional items such as grass seed, a colorful assortment of dried vegetables, shaved coconut, or biodegradable confetti. None of these need to be cleaned up, and are safe for the environment as well as any animals that live at your wedding site.

ATTIRE

Eco-Tip #12: Sport a Secondhand or Vintage Outfit

Employ the reduce, reuse, and recycle principle by wearing a secondhand or vintage outfit. The gown or suit can be easily altered to fit your body and style. When buying secondhand clothing, it's wise to exercise some caution. If possible, see the item in person to check for rips, stains, or irregularities. If the item will be shipped, don't be shy about asking for lots of photos from various angles. If possible, pay with a credit card or through a third-party payer in case you run into a problem.

Eco-Tip #13: Borrow a Gown or Suit from a Family Member

Many brides and grooms of weddings past put the time, effort, and cost into preserving their wedding day outfit, only to never pass it on to a child or other relative. Take a brief survey of relatives in your family who were married at least 5 years ago. Someone might have the perfect gown tucked away, just dying to be worn again. Many eco-friendly couples like the fact that wearing a relative's old gown or suit is more personal and intimate than buying one online.

Eco-Tip #14: Get Clothing Made from Organic Fabrics and Dyes

There's nothing wrong with buying a new gown or suit, but make your purchase green by opting for clothing made from organic and fair-trade fabrics, and with eco-friendly dyes or unbleached materials. Rawganique (www.rawganique.com) is one merchant that offers a wedding line made entirely from organic cotton, hemp, and linen. Threadhead Creations (www.threadheadcreations.com) also offers stunning wedding attire made from natural fibers like hemp, organic cotton, peace silk, and bamboo, and lets you design your own outfit if you don't like their off-the-rack selection.

Eco-Tip #15: Help Your Maids Get More Miles Out of Their Dresses

Don't force your bridesmaids to end up like Katherine Heigl's character in *27 Dresses*, who suffered with a full closet of dresses only worn once. Assign your bridesmaids gowns they will really want to sport again. The best way to do this is to decide on a color, then have your bridesmaids choose their own gowns from any retailer they want. They are likely to choose a cut, style, and shade that really appeals to them, and the variation in their choices will make your wedding party interesting and unique.

Eco-Tip #16: Think Outside the Dress

Instead of wearing a formal gown or tuxedo, don an outfit you are more likely to wear again, rather than one that will end up collecting dust in a stored garment bag. Brides might find re-wear possibilities in a simple white sundress. Grooms can choose a smart suit that can be worn to other weddings, job interviews, and other formal occasions. Getting married in an outfit you will wear again helps conserve energy, money, and saves on chemicals used in the gown-preservation process.

Eco-Tip #17: Avoid Polyester and Other Synthetic Materials

When purchasing clothes anew, avoid polyester, which is in most traditional wedding dresses. Making polyester is a resource-intensive process that requires a lot of water and energy. In addition, this synthetic fabric is made from petrochemicals, which are derived from oil and are a form of plastic. As such, it takes hundreds of years for polyester to break down. Seek clothes that aren't made of this unfriendly material. Also, look for veils made of natural peace silk organza rather than nylon tulle, another synthetic material.

Eco-Tip #18: Look for Cruelty-Free Fabrics and Cosmetics

Make sure no animals were harmed in the making of your wedding by avoiding clothing made from traditional silk. Silkworms are often boiled alive or electrocuted in order to make this product. Instead, opt for "peace silk," which is made from a cocoon after the silkworm has hatched and left it behind. Also, only buy clothes that have been made by a company that is known to not use child labor or overseas sweatshops. Finally, beautify with cosmetics that were not tested on animals.

Eco-Tip #19: Cut Down on One-Time-Use Items

A money-saving way to keep your wedding party green is to refrain from making your ushers and bridesmaids buy items they will only use at your wedding. For example, let bridesmaids buy black, silver, or gold shoes they will wear again, rather than asking them to get dyed matching ones. Avoid requiring maids to carry purses, scarves, parasols, or other items that won't match any other outfit. If there is an item you want everyone to have, see if it can be rented for the affair.

Eco-Tip #20: Wear a Brand New Recycled Dress

It is possible to wear a dress that is both recycled and brand new all at the same time. Partner with a dressmaker who will use factory scraps to make your dress. These pieces of fabric are often sent to the landfill, but technically are brand new and still useful. Or collect dresses from family members' wedding days past and have a dressmaker construct a new dress out of them. For decorative elements, have heirloom or vintage beaded necklaces, brooches, and pins incorporated into the design.

Eco-Tip #21: Donate Your Wedding Dress

It is romantic to think of your daughter one day walking down the aisle in the gown you wore. Yet in reality, very few brides are married in their mothers' dresses. Styles change quickly and most gowns don't appeal to brides of the future. Skip the gown preservation routine (and chemicals and costs associated with it) by donating your dress to charity. Brides Against Breast Cancer is a good choice— they resell your gown and donate the proceeds to benefit breast cancer patients and research.

Eco-Tip #22: Encourage Your Maids to Donate Their Dresses

Your bridesmaids should be encouraged to donate their gowns to any one of a number of charities that help bridesmaid dresses live on. Donatemydress.org is one nonprofit that provides donated dresses to underprivileged girls who need them for a prom or another special occasion. They have a national network of participating organizations and stores that make dropping off dresses a snap. Or your maids can simply donate their gowns to their local Goodwill or Salvation Army, where someone will invariably buy them as special occasion or costume fodder.

PHOTOGRAPHY

Eco-Tip #23: Hire a Green Photographer

Believe it or not, "green" photographers do exist and have sprung up in many cities. A green photographer will recycle the paper, packaging, and other items related to their business, as well as conserve water and energy in their studio. They will use rechargeable batteries and offer a line of wedding albums made from partially recycled content, avoiding limited dyes or toxic glues. Some even offer to donate a portion of their fee to an environmentally friendly cause related to photography (wildlife preservation, for example).

Eco-Tip #24: Go Digital

The environment is one of many reasons to shoot digital instead of film. Chemicals used to develop film are not eco-friendly, and photographers who print out proofs waste paper on a process that can be digitized. Select a photographer who will take digital pictures and create online galleries through which to view and order them.

VIDEOGRAPHY

Eco-Tip #25: Get a Green Videographer

Like green photographers, a green videographer will employ the principles of reduce, reuse, and recycle in every aspect of his or her business. A green videographer will recycle the materials related to their work, drive to jobs in an environmentally responsible vehicle, and conserve resources in their workspace. Plus, having your wedding digitally videotaped allows you to keep the guest list small. You can send copies of the ceremony to friends and family you weren't able to invite due to the high environmental cost of travel.

STATIONERY

Eco-Tip #26: What Is Eco-Friendly Stationery?

A lot of companies claim to make eco-friendly stationery. Know that truly green paper is made from at least 30 percent post-consumer content (i.e. recycled materials), but preferably 70 or 100 percent. It is often handmade and produced without acids or chlorine. It can come from a wood alternative, such as hemp. Environmentally friendly paper might be certified by the Forest Stewardship Council (FSC). Using one ton of 100 percent recycled paper saves 7,000 gallons of water, 17 trees, and enough energy to power a home for six months.

Eco-Tip #27: Narrow Your Stationery Needs

Take a minute to consider the various pieces of stationery involved in the average wedding. Most brides and grooms send or use all of the following: engagement announcements, save-the-date cards, shower invitations, shower thank you cards, wedding invitations (which include separate pieces of paper for RSVP cards and envelopes, driving directions, hotel information, and a weekend itinerary), ceremony programs, place cards, menu cards, wedding announcements, and thank you notes. For a more eco-friendly affair, aim to cut at least seven of these from your wedding and send virtual invites to the less formal festivities online instead.

Eco-Tip #28: Avoid Invitation Bling

Traditional wedding invitations are often dressed up in a festive but wasteful presentation of decorative tissue, ribbons, raffia, fake flowers, beads, glitter, and other elements. When choosing your invitations, skip this kind of bling, and also avoid invitations that feature multiple pieces of paper stacked on top of each other. Doing so can save approximately 24 trees per each ton of paper, and will also cut down on the amount of waste sent to a landfill and carbon dioxide that is spewed into the atmosphere.

Eco-Tip #29: Use Paper Alternatives

Investigate stationery made from a paper alternative—you will be amazed at the materials with which some companies work! Popular options include bamboo, hemp, banana stalks, cotton, elephant dung, flax, hemp, cloth, petals, flowers, silk, and grass. In addition to being handmade, acid and chlorine-free, as well as made from recycled products, many of these materials won't disintegrate or discolor with time, as wood pulp-based paper often does. Only your budget will limit your choice of the many paper alternatives on the market today.

Eco-Tip #30: Mind Your Ink

If you've chosen an eco-friendly paper for your stationery, remember that the ink you use makes a difference to the environment too. Look for companies that use organic inks or inks made from soy or vegetable-based materials. These are less harmful to the environment than typical petroleum-based inks. Vegetable-based printing inks include those made from canola, castor, linseed, safflower, and tung (Chinawood). Most vegetable-based inks are actually made from a blend of these ingredients, which allow printers to take advantage of each type's unique characteristics.

Eco-Tip #31: View the Envelope as Enemy

In addition to being another piece of paper to waste, envelopes often contain glue made from toxic materials that harm the environment in their creation. Aim to use as few envelopes as possible. Send save-the-date and thank you notes as postcards. Also, use postcards for RSVP cards (or go a step further and offer an email address where guests can send their responses). You can even turn your whole invitation into a postcard. Some companies print addresses directly on the back of your invitation, eliminating the need for an envelope entirely.

Eco-Tip #32: Clever Waste-Reducing Stationery Ideas

Use magnets as save-the-date notifications. These can feature a photo of you and your betrothed, and make a nice and useful keepsake for your guests. For invitations, seek out all-in-one varieties. These are invitations that fold up neatly into thirds, reducing the need for envelopes. On one third is the addressee's information; on another is the invitation itself. The final section holds an RSVP postcard that is neatly detachable by perforation. Check out the selection of all-in-one invitations at www. ForeverFiances.com.

Eco-Tip #33: Plant Your Stationery

For unique and elegant stationery, choose seed-embedded paper. This handmade, recycled paper is embedded with wildflower seeds. The invitation is torn up, planted in a pot or garden, and leaves behind nothing but festive blooms. An innovator of this stationery is Green Field Paper Company (www.greenfieldpaper.com). In addition to flower seed-embedded paper, Green Field offers invites made from recycled junk mail and paper infused with garlic skins or roasted coffee. Another company, Diva Entertains (www.divaentertains.com), offers plantable invitations, place cards, thank you notes, favors, and announcements.

Eco-Tip #34: Look Behind the Envelope

A lot of companies sell eco-friendly stationery, but not all are authentic. You will have found a truly green paper provider when the operation is a privately owned shop that gives a portion of its profits to charity. Some of its electricity will come from green sources such as hydro or solar power. Water used to make paper will be partially recycled, and they won't send bulky catalogues or drown you in samples. Their products will be printed on a digital press that does not emit Volatile Organic Compounds (VOCs).

Eco-Tip #35: Create a Wedding Website

Reduce the amount of excess paper delivered with your invitation by putting the details related to your wedding online, such as on WedSpace.com. WeddingWindow.com offers customized designs, as does EWedding.com, along with several other sites. Include the URL of your site with or on your wedding invitation. Then use the site to keep guests abreast of all information relating to the wedding, such as hotel options and information, directions, registry links, maps, rehearsal dinner information, nearby attractions, and more.

Eco-Tip #36: Go Paperless

The *San Francisco Chronicle* reported that the average cost of paper wedding invitations was $943. When you add postage to the mix, the cost of sending paper is well over a thousand bucks. Many couples are opting to save this money, and the resulting paper waste, by using electronic wedding invitations. Several companies offer e-wedding invitations that retain a sense of formality and propriety. For example, Greenvelope.com is one company that sends formal, individual digital invitations to each of your guests.

Eco-Tip #37: Manage the Party Online

Companies like Evite.com or MyPunchBowl.com let you send e-invitations, take stock of who's attending as well as what they might bring or do to help, and let you upload photos and send updates about your wedding. One interesting site is Pingg.com, which uses "surround-send" technology to send information to your guests via email, text, the web, and social messaging mediums like Facebook and Twitter. Though you might not associate these sites with weddings, more and more couples are using their convenient features to coordinate wedding-related events.

Eco-Tip #38: Use E-invites Only When Appropriate

For formal and large weddings, it remains appropriate to send a hard copy of an invitation. E-invitations can alienate older guests who are uncomfortable using the computer or who want the keepsake of an invitation. Secondly, the casual nature of e-invites is such that people can forget to respond to them. In these cases, reserve e-invitations for less formal announcements, such as save the dates. E-stationery is also good for festivities surrounding the wedding, such as the rehearsal dinner, the day-after brunch, or the bridal, bachelorette, and bachelor parties.

CATERING

Eco-Tip #39: Go Organic

Organic food is the mainstay of an environmentally friendly wedding. Because it hasn't been doused in chemicals, it tends to be more flavorful and colorful than conventionally grown food. Also, according to the Rodale Institute, it takes 30 percent less energy to grow, and doesn't pollute soil and groundwater with pesticides. Vegetarian menus have the least environmental impact, but if you do serve meat, choose organically fed, hormone-free meat raised at local ranches and farms. Also, opt for sustainably grown and fair-trade varieties of chocolate and coffee.

Eco-Tip #40: Know What's Local

There isn't much point in insisting that your caterer serves organic asparagus if it has to be flown in 5,000 miles from Argentina. The vegetables on the table may well be dumping more CO_2 into the environment than your guests did getting to your wedding! If the organic ingredients in your menu must come from afar, opt for conventionally yet locally grown produce. When food doesn't travel, it is better for the soil, air, and water, and benefits the local economy.

Eco-Tip #41: Craft a Seasonal Menu

Unless you are getting married in a very agricultural region, much of the produce in traditional dishes won't be in season and will be imported. Avoid causing your food to travel further than your guests by crafting a seasonal menu. In addition to being better for the environment, seasonal menus add flair, style, and theme to weddings. Seasonal menus do make it more difficult to taste food ahead of time, but ask your caterer to make sample dishes using substitute ingredients, such as peas for asparagus or potatoes for squash.

Eco-Tip #42: Seasonal Menu Suggestions — Winter

From a seasonal caterer's perspective, there is never a bad time to hold a wedding! If yours is booked for winter, you'll want to feature a hot soup instead of a salad course, and cider will be a nice addition to your coffee bar. Root vegetables, such as potatoes, turnips, parsnips, carrots, beets, rutabagas, and onions, are aromatic, tasty, and can be elegantly incorporated into several dishes. They pair especially well with grass-fed beef, free-range chicken, or hearty grains such as barley.

Eco-Tip #43: Seasonal Menu Suggestions — Spring

Though it is only the third most popular season in which to get married, caterers have a lot of fun with spring wedding dishes because of the fresh, young vegetables available at this time. Baby carrots, haricots verts, baby asparagus, new potatoes, and sugar snap peas are all springtime offerings that add color to a plate and flair to an appetizer. Rhubarb, pomegranates, mango, and apricots are also abundant this time of year and can be featured in salads, glazes, sauces, pies, cookies, or petits fours.

Eco-Tip #44: Seasonal Menu Suggestions — Summer

If you are getting married during summer, you're not alone—according to the Association of Bridal Consultants, the summer months account for around 40 percent of all weddings. Feature fresh fruit and vegetables in all your summer wedding dishes. Salads should include sliced berries, and if you serve a soup course, make sure it is chilled. Main dishes should be light and also incorporate fruit, such as grilled pears or pineapple. Be sure to add fresh lemonade to your drink menu, too.

Eco-Tip #45: Seasonal Menu Suggestions — Fall

Because of the crisp weather, gorgeous colors, and abundance of produce, fall is the second most popular season in which to hold a wedding. Like summer, you will have a bounty of items to choose from. For appetizers, consider baked brie and cranberry purses, or skewered butternut squash bites with a brown sugar glaze. A soothing pumpkin bisque served in hollowed-out bowls made from halved acorn squashes adds a wonderful touch to a soup course. Hot apple cider and miniature apple pies can be featured on your dessert table.

Eco-Tip #46: Be Ocean-Friendly

Only serve types of fish and seafood that are not overfished, endangered, or high in mercury. According to the Seafood Watch List, the following fishes are to be avoided: Chilean sea bass, Atlantic cod, king crab, mahi mahi, orange roughy, farmed Atlantic salmon, any type of shark or imported shrimp, bigeye or yellowfin tuna, and yellowtail. Better environmental bets are abalone, Alaska wild salmon, bay scallops, dungeness crab, skipjack tuna, white sea bass, rainbow trout, as well as farmed varieties of catfish, clams, mussels, and oysters.

Eco-Tip #47: Turn Your Caterer Green

In many cities it is difficult to find an all-organic caterer. But you can work with your caterer to tailor the menu to the environmental principles you've decided to incorporate into your wedding. Ask your caterer to shop at local farmer's markets and to choose fresh, seasonal, local and/or organic ingredients. Inquire as to whether they can substitute tofu, tempeh, seitan, or vegetables to make meat dishes vegetarian. You will find that most caterers want to earn your business and will work with you to meet your green needs.

Eco-Tip #48: Waste Not

Weddings are extravagant affairs, and with extravagance comes waste. Food is one of the most wasted items, because caterers don't want to run out of anything. Consider swapping plated meals for a buffet, which wastes less food since people take only what they want. If a buffet isn't elegant enough for your tastes, feature "meal stations" where dishes are made to order. Guests select what they want rather than being served a pre-set portion, which cuts down on the amount of uneaten food to be thrown away.

Eco-Tip #49: Donate Leftover Food

Ask your caterer to donate leftover food to a homeless shelter or soup kitchen. This will not always be possible, since it is illegal in some states to donate food that isn't canned, boxed, or otherwise sealed.

Likewise, health codes might prevent your reception site or caterer from providing already prepared food to another organization. If this is the case, ask your caterer to at least pack up the leftovers for you to deliver to an organization on your own or to feed out-of-town guests after the wedding.

Eco-Tip #50: Use Biodegradable Dishes

Serving more than 100 people appetizers, dinner, and dessert racks up a lot of dishes that need to be washed and dried, which wastes energy and water. Yet, you may have written off disposable dishes, thinking they will sit in a landfill long after death parts you and your loved one. Not so! Choose biodegradable plates and utensils made from potato, corn, or sugar cane. Most varieties are elegant looking and sturdy enough to keep your wedding from feeling like a picnic.

Eco-Tip #51: Leave Only Love Behind

Go the extra mile and aim to do without as many dishes as possible. Serve sushi or small appetizers in long cucumber cups, salad in hollowed-out melon bowls, and dips and salsas in pineapple halves. Soup, too, can be served in hollowed-out squash bowls, and plates can be fashioned out of sturdy, well-cleaned banana leaves. These options are most realistic for small weddings of under 50 people— but that size guest list is optimal for a truly eco-friendly wedding anyway.

Eco-Tip #52: Choose Eco-Friendly Table Settings

Make sure your tables are as earth-friendly as the food served on them. Set tables with organic cotton linens and napkins, or ones made from recycled or biodegradable materials. Rather than ordering plastic knickknacks made in China, use natural items to hold guest place cards, such as river rocks, sea shells, pine cones, small pumpkins. Or just print them out on small pieces of recycled stationery and attach them to a clothesline using wooden clothespins—this simple and eco-friendly set-up has a unique, organic look to it.

BAR

Eco-Tip #53: Drink as the Locals Do

Consuming locally is the new tenet of the environmental movement. When you consume products that are produced locally, you support small business and reduce the pollution and expense associated with long-distance shipping. With this in mind, serve a locally produced organic wine or beer at your wedding. Small-scale wineries have sprung up in surprising areas around the country, from Maine to Kentucky to Minnesota (see www.allamericanwineries.com for a complete list). Likewise, craft breweries are all the rage and many produce interesting and delicious beers at a great price.

Eco-Tip #54: Celebrate with Cork

When making beverage selections, choose wine bottles that have real corks. According to a report in the British newspaper, *The Independent*, the increasing use of screw-top bottles has driven down the demand for cork—and subsequently, its price. As a result, farmers in some areas of the world are using unsustainable farming methods to harvest cork because it saves them money to do so. Choose cork to protect farmers and forests.

Eco-Tip #55: Avoid the Bottle and Can
When interviewing catering companies and bartenders, ask if they can serve tap water and fountain drinks rather than bottled waters or sodas. Likewise, look into getting a keg of beer that can be served on tap, rather than offering individual bottles. Your goal is to reduce the number of bottles and cans that need to be used. If bottles and cans are unavoidable, set up recycling bins near the bar and make sure the venue you select takes them to be recycled.

PARTY FAVORS

Eco-Tip #56: Avoid Disposable Cameras
Disposable cameras are a green wedding no-no. For one, harsh, hazardous chemicals are used in film development, and disposable means—well, disposable. Secondly, most of your guests will have their own digital cameras and will probably email photos to you. If you want the fun of disposables without the environmental harm, set up a laptop with a memory card reader that your guests can use as a group photo station. They can upload their pictures on-site, and you'll have a complete collection by the time you're on your way to the bridal suite.

Eco-Tip #57: Offer Eco-Friendly Favors
Rather than spending money on plastic favors that your guests might throw away or leave behind, offer them small gifts that reflect your commitment to the environment. Look for favors made from organic, recycled, or biodegradable materials. Small food items, such as fair-trade chocolates, coffee, or candies, make nice eco-friendly favors, and often come in attractive, recycled packages with your name and wedding date printed on them. Many such favors are available online for less than $5 each.

Eco-Tip #58: Give Your Guests the Gift of Charity
Eco-friendly brides and grooms are increasingly forgoing party favors and opting to make a donation to charity instead. Pick any charity you and your partner care about—for the comfort of your guests, choose an environmental, social, or medical one rather than a political one. On recycled or plantable paper, print cards that let your guests know you are donating in their honor in lieu of a traditional favor. These can double as table setting cards too. Spread your money around by assigning each table a different charity.

Eco-Tip #59: Carbon Offset Your Wedding
The average wedding emits approximately 14.5 tons of CO_2 into the atmosphere. When you consider that the average person emits 12 tons of CO_2 over the course of a whole year, it becomes clear that weddings leave a heavy carbon footprint. Counteract the carbon impact of your wedding by giving your guests carbon offset credits instead of favors. These can be purchased from organizations such as Climate Care or TerraPass.com, which use the money to fund eco-friendly projects that fight climate change.

MUSIC

Eco-Tip #60: Use Live Musicians Who Play Acoustically

Using amplified or recorded music adds to your wedding's electrical footprint. Plus, DJs and bands with large amplifiers, microphones, and bundles of wiring tend to drive low-mileage vans or trucks to lug around their heavy equipment. Avoid this scene by hiring live musicians who play acoustically (unplugged). For ceremonies, consider harpists, string, or wind ensembles. For receptions, brass, bluegrass, or country bands get the party started. In addition to being eco-friendly, unamplified music keeps decibel levels low, making it easy and comfortable for your guests to talk to each other.

BAKERY

Eco-Tip #61: Skip Dessert Plates

Minimize the number of dishes used during your wedding by making the dessert course a finger food-only event. Offer bite-sized, plate-less desserts, such as cupcakes, cookies, brownies, or petits fours. Your guests will only need to use recycled or cloth napkins to wipe the delicious crumbs from their lips! Further reduce the amount of waste by creating a dessert bar where guests can go up and get what they want, rather than being served a pre-set assortment that might go uneaten.

Eco-Tip #62: Enlist a Friend to Act as Baker

Rather than hiring a professional to bake your wedding cake, ask a friend to bake one for you. Baking a cake or cupcakes in a home stove consumes much less energy than a professional commercial oven. Plus, you have control over which ingredients are used, and can therefore select free-range eggs and organic milk, sugar, and flour. By transporting the cake to the reception in a private car, you cut down on the energy consumed by a chilled delivery truck. Whichever friend you ask will be honored to give you this special and delicious gift.

Eco-Tip #63: Eco-Friendly Cake Toppers

Don't bother with a generic throwaway cake topper made from plastic. Top your cake with something biodegradable but decorative, such as edible flower petals, leaves, or candies. Also, forgo any cake decorations made from inorganic materials, such as fake pearls. Most quality bakers can make elegant cake decorations such as seashells, flowers, or leaves from sugar that are completely edible—and delicious.

Eco-Tip #64: Put Yourself on Your Cake

Only buy a cake topper if it is something you will love to look at forever. A fantastic example comes from WeBobble.com, a company that makes sculpted cake topper bobblehead dolls that look exactly like you and your partner. You send them a photograph, and they create three-dimensional dolls that you and your partner will love to keep on display in your home long after your cake has been eaten. CustomBobble.com offers a similar product you won't ever want to throw out.

Eco-Tip #65: Serve a Vegan Dessert

Go a step further than finding a baker who makes organic desserts—find one who specializes in vegan ones. A vegan diet is arguably the most environmentally friendly diet around because it cuts out all animal products (the production of which are very resource-intensive). Serve a cake that has been made without milk or eggs to really reduce your dessert's carbon footprint. The good news is that most professional vegan bakers create such delicious treats, you'll never know the difference.

Eco-Tip #66: What's Holding Your Cake Together?

Traditional tiered wedding cakes are usually held together with metal, plastic tubing, and other inorganic materials, most of which go straight to the trash. Avoid this waste by serving either a sheet cake or cupcakes. If you must have a tiered wedding cake, talk with your baker about returning the cake structure materials so they can be washed and reused in someone else's cake. Also, instead of showcasing your cake on a plastic plate wrapped in cloth and decorated with ribbon, try a festive, reusable bamboo platter instead.

Eco-Tip #67: Rent a Cake

A lavish wedding cake is part of any bride's dream, but their production and delivery are expensive and not always eco-friendly. Have your cake and eat it too by renting a fake wedding cake! RenttheCakeofYourDreams.com makes realistic-looking fake cakes you can rent for a fraction of the price. These fakes even contain a space for actual cake so you can still have a traditional cake cutting. Afterwards, the fake is whisked away and your caterer will serve a sheet cake that's been cut behind the scenes. Renting a cake is an unusual but eco-friendly way to reduce waste without sacrificing style.

FLOWERS

Eco-Tip #68: Choose Organic Flowers

If you can afford it, use organic flowers to brighten your ceremony and reception sites. These will have been grown without pesticides or insecticides. Although your guests won't be ingesting the flowers, any plants grown with pesticides or insecticides take a toll on the environment by polluting groundwater and soil. Start by checking out OrganicBouquet.com, the first online organic-flower vendor, which has been operating since 2001. They work with both local and national stores to get you organic flowers at a reasonable price.

Eco-Tip #69: If You Buy Organic, Coordinate With Your Florist

Because organic flowers are not preserved in the same way conventionally grown flowers are, they don't last as long. Therefore, if you decide to go organic, your florist will need to be on top of ordering, delivery, and arrangement schedules so you don't end up with wilted or browning flowers. Also, if your florist is unfamiliar with working with organics, let him or her know to look either for the USDA Certified Organics emblem or the VeriFlora seal (the first green certification standard for the floral industry).

Eco-Tip #70: Get Locally Grown Flowers

Many commercially grown flowers sold in the U.S. actually aren't grown here—many come from Latin American countries where they tend to be sprayed with chemicals that are banned or unregistered in the U.S. Plus, shipping them in chilled cargo containers uses an enormous amount of fuel. So even if you choose to buy non-organic flowers, choose ones that have been locally grown. Check out offerings at your local nursery or wholesale flower shop, and always ask where your flowers were grown.

Eco-Tip #71: Let Your Flowers Live On

If organic cut flowers are too rich for your budget, use commercially grown potted plants and flowers. Encourage your guests to take them home, where they can continue to enjoy them or put them in the ground. Be aware that not all of your guests will take home potted plants, however—especially those who have traveled long distances. If you have several pots left over, plant them in your garden or a community garden, and enjoy these physical reminders of your wedding year after year.

Eco-Tip #72: Decorate Seasonally

Demanding tulips at your February wedding is going to cost both you and the environment. As with your menu, decorating your wedding with seasonally available plants and flowers saves money and is easier on the earth. And you still have many luxurious options at your fingertips! Winter weddings can be festively decorated with cranberries, pine cones, lemon leaf garlands, and sprigs of holly and mistletoe. Likewise, autumn weddings can feature a rich array of golds, browns, and oranges, and floral arrangements should include small decorative pumpkins, seed pods, and leaves.

Eco-Tip #73: One Set of Flowers Can Serve Two Weddings

Caring about the environment means going out of your way to reduce, reuse, and recycle. With this mantra in mind, consider sharing your flowers with another couple getting married the same day. If you've booked your wedding in a ballroom, hotel, restaurant, or historical property, chances are someone is getting married either just before or just after you. Get this person's name and talk with them about their color scheme and preferences. It may be possible to split the financial and environmental costs that flowers incur.

Eco-Tip #74: A Flower's After Party

The flowers that bring romance to a wedding often end up in the trash by the time the couple reaches the honeymoon suite. Instead of sending them to the landfill, have your flowers composted after the wedding. Or have them dried and turned into decorative potpourri bags (if these are small enough, include them with the thank you cards you send to your guests). Finally, donate your flowers to a local institution that may need brightening up, such as a hospital, funeral home, or elderly care center.

Eco-Tip #75: Save the Oasis for Your Honeymoon

Organic flowers? Check. Dried or reusable arrangement accessories? Check. The only thing left for a totally eco-friendly floral arrangement is to avoid using oasis foam—the green squishy brick florists soak in water and use to showcase arrangements. Oasis foam is made from plastic and is not biodegradable, so ask your florist to work with something less toxic. For example, hold flowers together with vines that are wrapped tightly around flower stems. These become part of the arrangement design and can be dried or composted with the flowers after the wedding.

Eco-Tip #76: Make Your Flowers Work a Double Shift

Whether you use cut flowers, potted plants, or flower alternatives, make sure your arrangements do double duty by being at both your ceremony and reception. Depending on how far these are from each other, this can be tricky but worth it. Having one set of arrangements cuts down on both the cost and the amount needed (and thus wasted). Ask your wedding coordinator to work with your florist and caterer so that they can move arrangements from the ceremony to the reception site during the cocktail hour, when guests will be busy.

Eco-Tip #77: Use Nature as Your Decoration

Minimize the need for flowers entirely by holding your ceremony or reception somewhere already richly decorated with plants. Botanical gardens, museums, historical sites, beaches, and fields all tend to be well-equipped with plants you don't have to pay for, set up, or tear down. Also, consider having your wedding at a nonprofit organization's retreat or camp. In addition to being located in nature, your guests can all spend the night, making your wedding a multi-day celebration.

DECORATIONS

Eco-Tip #78: Watch What You Toss

There are several eco-friendly alternatives to tossing rice, flower petals, or confetti during your ceremony. Instead of confetti (which is made with bleaches and dyes) or rice (which is banned from some venues due to the difficulty in cleaning it up) you can use grass seed, flower seeds, or shaved coconut. These natural items often come wrapped in attractive, recyclable baggies. If you have your heart set on confetti, check out an eco-friendly kind called Ecofetti. It's made from biodegradable materials that dissolve quickly and easily in water.

Eco-Tip #79: Make Centerpieces Out of Reusable Items

Your wedding can be made more earth-friendly by making your centerpieces out of items that will have a life beyond the party. Build centerpieces from materials you are sure to reuse, such as ribbon, fabric, paper lanterns, baskets, pots, glass bowls, and candleholders. Make personalized centerpieces out of framed pictures of your guests or images from your life with your partner that you can later use as décor around your home. Invite your guests to pilfer the centerpieces and take what they think they will use.

Eco-Tip #80: Edible Centerpiece Ideas

Centerpieces made from edible items are eco-friendly, cost-effective, and unique! Gorgeous, lavish centerpieces can be made using heirloom vegetables, lush bouquets of herbs, and colorful fruits. These can be arranged in terra cotta pots, vases or vintage bowls, or on platters. Tiered cupcakes and cookies also make a festive centerpiece. These centerpieces can be intended for your guests to eat or just feature items you plan to take home to use in your kitchen.

Eco-Tip #81: Use Eco-Friendly Candles

Using candles cuts down on the electricity used to light up your wedding. When selecting candles, avoid cheap, environmentally hazardous ones made from paraffin-based wax, which is a petroleum by-product. Also, skip artificially scented candles—these often have wicks that release chemicals into the air. Instead, choose cotton-wicked candles made from soy, beeswax, or vegetable-based oils. These materials are renewable, sustainable, biodegradable, water-soluble, and non-toxic. Plus, they last longer than wax candles since they burn at lower temperatures.

Eco-Tip #82: Cruise Thrift Stores for Your Decorations

Who said centerpieces had to be expensive? You can craft lovely, intricate, and unique ones out of materials found in thrift stores. Most Salvation Army or Goodwill shops carry a wide assortment of glass bowls, vases, platters, jars, and other reclaimed items. Not only are these items inexpensive, but you'll be supporting a charity and incorporating recycling into your wedding all at the same time. The fact that they won't match will only enhance the artistry of such creations. After your wedding, re-donate the items so someone else can use them.

TRANSPORTATION

Eco-Tip #83: Opt for Eco-Friendly Wedding Party Transportation

Traditional weddings typically feature gas-guzzlers, such as limousines and flashy SUV or Hummer limos. But shuttling your bridal party around doesn't have to pollute the environment, and you can still do so in style. Check out green transportation services websites local to your area. Many let you reserve luxury fuel-efficient and alternative vehicles, and even provides chauffeurs to drive them. The rentable fleet includes high-end eco-friendly models by Mercedes, Lexus, Toyota, Ford, and Chevy. Some of the available vehicles are hybrids, while others get exceptionally good gas mileage.

Eco-Tip #84: Get Your Guests Together

The average wedding has around 140 guests. Assuming most guests come in pairs, around 70 cars will be driving first to your ceremony site and then to your reception. To cut down on the CO_2 your guests release as they share in your special day, consider renting a bus to get them from place to place. It cuts down on pollution, and you won't have to print individual driving directions, or worry anyone will be late to the party. Or hold your ceremony and reception in the same place.

Eco-Tip #85: Getting the Bride and Groom Around

Just because you and your betrothed care about the environment doesn't mean you have to sacrifice style. There are many ways to get from ceremony to reception or from reception to bridal suite that are both decadent and eco-friendly. Go pre-industrial and choose unmotorized transportation for and your partner. A pedicab is a great option—this is a rickshaw or bike taxi that can be spruced up with organic flowers, recycled lace, a white awning, or other festive decorations. Another romantic and eco-friendly option is a horse-and-buggy.

Eco-Tip #86: Avoid Destination Weddings

While it is increasingly popular for couples to choose organic flowers and recycled decorations, many don't realize their wedding causes the most environmental damage when their guests travel to get there. Consider that more than 4,400 pounds of CO_2 are released into the atmosphere when just one person takes a cross-country flight. How many of your guests do you think will fly to attend your wedding? To reduce the number in the air, avoid destination weddings which require everyone—including you and your partner—to fly.

Eco-Tip #87: Offset Guest Travel with Carbon Credits

If air travel can't be avoided, absorb the impact of your guests' travel by buying carbon offset credits. To calculate how much carbon dioxide is expended by your guests' trip, check out TerraPass's wedding calculator (www.terrapass.com/wedding). For example, let's say 20 guests are flying from New York to attend your wedding in San Francisco. In doing so, they will generate about 41,000 pounds of CO_2. It would cost you a mere $243.95 to offset this damage—and you get a framed certificate acknowledging your contribution to the planet.

RENTAL ITEMS & GIFTS

Eco-Tip #88: Give Love, Get Love

Gifts are part of the fun of getting married but many newlyweds end up with random candy dishes and ugly gravy boats. To get something more meaningful from your guests, ask them to donate to their favorite charity instead of buying you a gift. Encourage them to think creatively, such as planting a tree or sponsoring a child in your name. Some guests, however, will insist on getting you a traditional gift. To appease them, create a small registry that only has the essentials on it.

Eco-Tip #89: Register for Change

Another approach to donation-based gifts is to create a charitable gift registry. These work the same way regular registries do—but instead of registering for things, couples encourage their guests to donate to charity. Just like an in-store registry, gift givers can browse the couple's wish list and donate to causes they've selected. When selecting organizations, stick to groups that serve nature, animals, disease prevention, or relief efforts. Check out Changingthepresent.org, which lets you specify charities your guests can "shop" at. Globalgiving.com also has a charitable registry option.

Eco-Tip #90: Tithe Your Gifts

It is rare that newlyweds don't need any new things. After all, this is the start of your life together, and you might want some special items to remember it by. While charitable registries work for couples who don't need gifts (or who have been together for long enough that they have already purchased most everything they need), newer couples probably need help. In this case, consider donating 10 percent of the gift checks you get to charity. Or donate 10 percent of the merchandise you receive.

Eco-Tip #91: Ask for the Gift of Experience

Rather than registering for a lasagna pan or new sheets, ask for experience-based gifts you can enjoy during the first year of your marriage. Ask for an annual pass or membership to a local zoo, aquarium, wildlife park, nature conservancy, or nonprofit organization. Request a series of tickets to local plays, live music, or sporting events. In some areas it is possible to register for delivery service of organic food grown by local farmers. In addition to being fun, these gifts keep your receipt of "stuff" to a minimum.

Eco-Tip #92: Register for Eco-Friendly Gifts

Receive traditional gifts with a nontraditional twist by registering with the growing number of companies devoted to selling eco-friendly goods. Check out sites like Greenfeet.com, Re-modern. com, Gaiam.com, or Greensage.com where you can register for eco-friendly tableware, linens, and home accessories. Or, try the AlternativeGiftRegistry.org. This site allows you to collect various eco-friendly items from any website and display them in one searchable registry.

Eco-Tip #93: Pick Up Gifts Yourself

If you do register for gifts, ask that they be held for in the store for pickup. This will prevent them from being shipped to you, which wastes packaging materials, unnecessary gift wrapping, postage, and shipping and handling fees, not to mention the fuel it takes to drive delivery trucks around. Since many couples end up returning or exchanging gift items anyway, it makes environmental sense to ask the stores at which you register to hold any gifts purchased off your registry, rather than mailing them.

Eco-Tip #94: Get Gifts for Life

Perhaps you and your partner, like many newlyweds, are planning to move in together or buy your first home after the wedding. Ask guests to contribute to this next phase of your life by registering for eco-friendly home materials, such as solar panels, Energy Star roofing materials, or a water recycling system. Such gifts aren't glamorous or traditional but they speak loudly toward your commitment to the environment as a couple. Set up an online fund where guests can collectively contribute the money needed to buy such materials.

BRIDESMAID & USHER GIFTS

Eco-Tip #95: Eco-Friendly Bridesmaid Gift Ideas

Your options are endless! Narrow them down by presenting your bridesmaids with something green they will also use during the ceremony. Gift them eco-friendly makeup or organic cotton scarves they can wear around their shoulders when the sun sets over your wedding. Get them matching necklaces, bracelets, or anklets that come from a jeweler who works exclusively with recycled materials, such as reclaimed metal, sea glass, or real shells. Gift certificates for a facial with an esthetician who works with organic products will be much appreciated too.

Eco-Tip #96: Charitable Bridesmaid Gift Ideas

Give your maids something that helps others. Many nonprofit organizations now offer eco-friendly, fair-trade gifts made by disadvantaged women who live locally, nationally, and internationally. For example, GlobalGirlfriend.com sells purses, jewelry, totes, bath products, and clothing made by struggling women in Asia, Africa, and Latin America. To help women closer to home, check out the WomensBeanProject.com, a nonprofit social enterprise in Denver that keeps women out of poverty by selling lovely handmade gift baskets stocked with fair-trade, organic soups, coffees, and spices.

Eco-Tip #97: Eco-Friendly Usher Gift Ideas

Eco-friendly gift ideas abound for your ushers too. Consider wallets or belts made from hemp, or beer steins made from recycled glass. Monogrammed organic cotton towels make a classy gift, as do cuff links made from reclaimed materials. Peruse GreenAmerica.org to get more ideas. If your men are into sports, look into getting them biodegradable golf tees and water-soluble balls from EcoGolf.com, or fair-trade eco-friendly soccer, football, and basketballs from FairTradeSports.com. The proceeds from each purchase go to children's charities.

Eco-Tip #98: Show Your Ushers A Good Time

Forgo foisting more stuff upon your ushers and get them an experience-based gift, such as sports ticket packages, concert tickets, or season passes to a local events venue. Most guys will also appreciate a beer-of-the-month club or tasting membership at an organic, local brewery. Add a charitable twist by including a membership to the clean water organization, Surfrider Foundation (www.surfrider.org), in with their gift—and get one for yourself as well.

Eco-Tip #99: Present Your Bridal Party with Gifts in a Gift

No matter what you give your bridal party, wrap it in something other than flashy wrapping paper. Use newspaper that bears the date of your wedding, and tie it off with twine or hemp rope. Put gifts inside recycled gift bags. Start collecting bags now, and you'll have plenty by the time of your wedding. Or skip paper entirely and wrap gifts in swatches of cloth, which afterwards can be sewn together as a wedding keepsake quilt or napkin set.

HONEYMOON PLANNING

Eco-Tip #100: Be a "Voluntourist"

See the world and do something good by taking a volunteer honeymoon. Volunteering can be the focus of your trip, or be just a day's activity. For example, couples might incorporate work in Tsunami-affected areas into a vacation to Japan or Thailand. They might volunteer to do a one-day beach cleanup in Hawaii or spend a week helping protect sea turtle mating territory in Costa Rica. Many couples are not the lounge-on-the-beach type anyway, and volunteer vacations have seen a boom in recent years.

Eco-Tip #101: Take an Ecotour

According to the World Tourism Organization, ecotourism is the fastest growing market in the tourism industry. Ecotourism is travel that features low-impact, small-scale exploration and appreciation of a fragile or protected area. Ecotours work to educate travelers about social and environmental challenges to the area, and their profits are put back into local communities. They sometimes include home stays with local families and never feature chain hotels, restaurants, or activities that harm or exploit the local culture or environment.

Eco-Tip #102: Stay at an Eco-Friendly Resort

Eco-friendly resorts are increasingly popular. These are lodges built from environmentally friendly and locally available materials. They make efforts to conserve water, electricity, and minimize waste. While some eco-resorts don't have amenities like TV or air conditioning, others find amazing ways to deliver luxury while remaining green. Check out Six Senses resorts (www.sixsenses.com), which feature towel-reuse, recycling, and composting programs, and use renewable energy, including energy-efficient light bulbs, biodiesel, solar and wind power, and deep-sea cooling. Spas feature only natural ingredients and restaurants serve locally grown organic produce.

Eco-Tip #103: Honeymoon Close to Home

According to the Condé Nast Bridal Group, 90 percent of the 2.3 million couples who marry each year in the U.S. take a honeymoon—and they take a flight to get there. But remember that flying causes CO_2 to be released into the atmosphere, and the longer the flight, the more of it. To lessen your honeymoon's carbon footprint, take a trip somewhere close to home. If you can't avoid flying, restrict how many flights you will take (avoid taking inter-island flights, for example).

Eco-Tip #104: Compensate the Environment for the Cost of Your Honeymoon

If you didn't buy carbon offsets to make up for guest travel or to use as party favors, definitely carbon offset your honeymoon. Carbon offset services are provided by Climate Care (www.climatecare.org), Carbon Fund (www.carbonfund.org), Sustainable Travel International (www.sustainabletravelinternational.org), or CO2Balance (www.co2balance.com). Or plant trees to compensate for your travels. A flight from Houston to Hawaii uses about as much carbon per passenger as a fully-grown tree can absorb in a year. So plant a few trees to make up for the carbon used by your trip.

Eco-Tip #105: Be a Green Tourist

No matter where you go or how you get there, once you have arrived at your honeymoon destination, make an effort to be an eco-friendly tourist. This means patronizing locally owned shops and restaurants that feature organic, handmade products and foods. Book accommodations that are centrally located so you can get around on foot or bike rather than by rental car. Engage in tourist activities that benefit the local economy and environment. Above all, take only pictures and leave only footprints.

Top 10 Trends, Ideas & Resources

Karen French

TOP 10 TRENDS, IDEAS & RESOURCES

WHILE THE INTERNET IS A WONDERFUL TOOL WHEN PLANNING A WEDDING, it can also seem like an endless parade of options and choices when it comes to vendors, ideas, and inspiration. Learning to self-edit when choosing your wedding décor and theme is one of the toughest parts of wedding planning.

This section offers a series of fun Top 10 lists on every aspect of wedding planning, from the most inspirational wedding blogs, to the top things to do with your wedding gown after the big day, to a list of the most overplayed wedding songs you still probably love.

These lists will help you get an at-a-glance look at some of the very best ideas, trends, destinations, resources, vendors, designers, and more.

This chapter should make you smile while you get inspiration for having the wedding of your dreams. Don't be overwhelmed by the many choices available. Have fun and enjoy every step of the planning process. It's your chance to plan the party of your dreams!

TOP 10 ATTIRE & ACCESSORIES TRENDS

Cowboy boots

Brides wanting to show personal style are going with the casual-cool look of cowboy boots under their wedding dresses. Brides may wear heels for the ceremony and change into boots for the reception. An outdoor wedding on soft ground, for instance, will be tough to navigate in heels, but cowboy boots are chic and comfortable.

Mismatched bridesmaids' dresses

Have a perfectly un-put-together wedding party by choosing one color and letting your bridesmaids pick their own dresses. Brides can also choose the specific dress style and have their 'maids pick their own color from a variety of hues. The benefits? Your ladies get to pick a dress in their price range, find something that looks great on them, select a dress they really will want to wear again, and express their personal style.

Short wedding gowns

The sweeping train of a long gown isn't for every bride. Tea-length hems—or even shorter—are showing up on brides everywhere looking for less formal gowns, particularly for outdoor or warm weather weddings, or for a more relaxed, party-style reception look. The best part? Brides can show off a great pair of shoes.

Colorful shoes

Want to infuse color into your wedding attire? Consider a colorful pair of shoes. Bright blue, hot pink, fire-engine red, leaf green, and sunny yellow are becoming increasingly popular. A pop of color is unexpected and fun and makes for fantastic photos.

Shrugs, capes, cardigans and boleros

Even summer weddings will have cool evenings that require some sort of cover-up. While wraps and pashminas are traditional, brides are getting creative with custom-designed shrugs, capes, and boleros with beading, ruffles, and other detailing. Many wedding designers also create these pieces to match their gowns. A colorful cardigan is another great way to look chic and stay cozy.

Large flower headpieces

Traditional bridal tiaras are taking a backseat to beautiful floral headpieces as of late. Countless stores, including those on Etsy.com, are selling bold custom flowers to be worn as headbands, clips, and more for the bride. If you plan to wear a veil for the ceremony, you can replace it with a flower headpiece for the reception.

Birdcage veils

The vintage look of the birdcage veil has become a huge trend in bridal accessories. With this veil, a simple piece of lace or French netting covers the eyes or the face, attached with a fastener, for a look that is beautiful, classic, and elegant.

Sequined or beaded sashes and belts

A simple dress can get a stylish upgrade in a fast and inexpensive way with the addition of a sequined or beaded sash or belt. Search through online craft boutiques like those on Etsy.com for gorgeous handmade versions.

Bold, chunky necklaces

Bridal jewelry has traditionally been dainty and delicate—a thin necklace or strand of pearls. However, bold, chunky necklaces are making a big statement these days, and are especially beautiful with a simple gown. Just keep other jewelry, makeup, and hair accessories minimal.

Bouquet made out of vintage brooches

Want a bouquet that you can cherish forever and that won't wilt an hour after the reception? An incredible trend is having a bouquet custom-created out of vintage brooches and pins. Have the women in your family contribute their own pieces, and an artist can wire them together to make a bouquet that is totally unique, personal, and a lifelong memento.

TOP 10 MODERN WEDDING SONGS

* "Lucky," Jason Mraz & Colbie Caillat
* "Make You Feel My Love," Adele
* "Marry Me," Train
* "I'm Yours," Jason Mraz
* "Today," Joshua Radin
* "Rhythm of Love," Plain White T's
* "Just the Way You Are," Bruno Mars
* "You and Me," Lifehouse
* "Better Together," Jack Johnson
* "Forever," Ben Harper

TOP 10 WEDDING INSPIRATION BLOGS

Once Wed, oncewed.com

Once Wed began as one of the first and only free online resources for buying and selling wedding gowns. The site has now expanded to include everything from real weddings and inspiration galleries to modern DIY wedding projects.

Ruffled Blog, ruffledblog.com

Ruffled celebrates the savvy vintage bride with a collection of witty perspectives and clever ideas to inspire unique style. It's smart, sassy and hip to the latest trends, with a hint of sophistication for those looking to stand out among the crowd.

Style Me Pretty, stylemepretty.com
Style Me Pretty is a style-savvy wedding resource that features only the most chic and style-centric wedding content, and is continually discovering new and talented vendors and brides with an eye for all things gorgeous.

Green Wedding Shoes, greenweddingshoes.com
Featuring Southern California wedding inspiration for the modern bride, this blog highlights real weddings that incorporate a special touch—a unique theme, beautiful setting, or memorable details.

Southern Weddings Blog, swsmag.net
At this online extension of the print edition of *Southern Weddings Magazine,* the editors hand-pick content and showcase the top real weddings, professionals, products and wedding news daily.

100 Layer Cake, 100layercake.com/blog
100 Layer Cake is a wedding planning resource for thoughtful, crafty, modern women. Vendors, DIY projects, and weddings are hand-picked and thoroughly researched by the creators of the blog.

Snippet & Ink, snippetandink.blogspot.com
Snippet & Ink is perhaps most well known for its colorful inspiration boards, but special giveaways, real weddings, budget-friendly ideas, décor, tablescapes, and more make this a daily stop for inspiration.

Kiss the Groom.com, kissthegroom.com
Created by renowned photographer, Elizabeth Messina, Kiss the Groom celebrates weddings, family and other love stories through photographs and personal insights.

Something Old, Something New, kenziekate.blogspot.com
Creator and designer of KenzieKate Invitations posts daily products and inspiration for modern weddings and parties.

The Wedding Chicks, weddingchicks.com
Everything new, classic, funky, hip and just plain fun for weddings. Wedding Chicks will fill your days with inspiration and beauty or help you find that perfect vendor.

TOP 10 PHOTOGRAPHY TRENDS

Proposal caught on film
One of the sweetest trends in photography is hiring a photographer to capture the proposal on film. This is a wonderful surprise and memories you'll want to show family and friends and look back on for years.

First Look photos

Traditionally, it was bad luck for the bride and groom to sneak a peek before the ceremony. Today, many couples opt to see each other before they walk down the aisle. Not only does a "First Look" alleviate some of the pre-wedding jitters, but these are some of the most special moments of the entire day. Have your photographer capture the magic that happens when the groom turns around and sees his wife-to-be for the first time, looking more beautiful than he could have imagined. The happiness, hugs, and tears are priceless!

Day-after shoots

Day-after shoots offer the bride and groom a unique chance to take some intimate bridal shots together when they're totally relaxed, and without taking them away from their wedding guests and reception. It also lets the couple pose in any location they want. So put your gown and tux back on and have a day-after session!

Trash the Dress

Jump in the ocean, roll around in the dirt, climb a tree, have a snowball fight. Trash the Dress sessions are great for brides who don't get sentimental about saving their gowns and want a set of fun, unique and often sexy photos after the wedding. If you can't imagine ruining your wedding dress but love the Trash the Dress concept, purchase a second, less-expensive gown for the shoot.

Engagement shoots with props

Engagement shoots have moved far beyond the old-fashioned studio portrait to include a complete photo shoot with wardrobe changes, location changes and fun props. Anything goes but consider balloons, masks, books, bubbles, hula hoops, cotton candy, lollipops, swing sets, roller coasters, and more to make your engagement shoot amazing.

Shooting in film

While digital film has become the norm in the wedding industry, a few top photographers, including wedding superstar, Jose Villa, have declared themselves "100 percent film." Film forces the photographer to choose and set up each shot carefully and artfully, and produces a timeless, romantic and textured photo. Additionally, many photographers shoot a combination of both film and digital, so you get the best of both worlds.

Coffee table book of images

In addition to purchasing a professional wedding album from your photographer, you might make your own coffee table-style book. Companies like Blurb.com offer stylish, totally customizable hardcover books that start at less than $25.

Show a ceremony slideshow at the reception

Have your photographer create a slideshow of images that he or she takes during the ceremony and shows during the reception. You will love seeing your ceremony shots paired with a traditional slideshow of classic photos of you growing up and as a couple.

Boudoir sessions
Give your husband-to-be a sexy wedding present he'll cherish forever—a set of pictures taken at a boudoir photography studio or in your home. Special lingerie, sexy but tasteful poses, and hair and makeup styling make this a sensual and intimate gift.

Using engagement pictures as Save the Date cards
Turn engagement shoot images into personalized Save the Date cards your guests will want to display and keep. Magnets can also save money on ordering traditional stationery cards.

TOP 10 MOST OVERPLAYED WEDDING SONGS (THAT YOU STILL MIGHT LOVE)

* "Celebration," Kool and the Gang
* "Shout," Isley Brothers
* "The Electric Slide," Various artists
* "Dancing Queen," ABBA
* "Brick House," Commodores
* "You Shook Me," AC/DC
* "YMCA," Village People
* "Chicken Dance," Werner Thomas
* "Old Time Rock N Roll," Bob Seeger
* "Conga," Gloria Estefan

TOP 10 THINGS TO DO WITH YOUR GOWN POST-WEDDING

Shorten it into a summer dress
Depending on the cut, material and detailing of your dress you may be able to have it shortened into a gorgeous summer dress. Hire a talented seamstress you trust to create this second look from your gown.

Donate to Brides Against Breast Cancer
Donate your dress to this organization, which then sells them at events around the country. Proceeds help grant final wishes to men and women with terminal breast cancer, as well as create awareness and outreach for the disease.

Give it to a friend or family member
Do you know a friend or family member who might benefit from wearing your gown? Maybe she is on a very tight budget or just really loved your dress. It can be a wonderful gesture to give your gown

to a loved one.

OnceWed.com or PreOwnedWeddingDresses.com
Sell your gown secondhand on one of these two trusted sites. Listings are free on OnceWed.com, and PreOwnedWeddingDresses.com charges only a small one-time listing fee and does not take a cut of your dress sale. Give your gown a happy home!

Have it preserved
You may want to have your gown preserved for your children or grandchildren or to look at over the years and remember your wedding day. Preservation includes cleaning a dirty hem and any perspiration, champagne or sugar stains, which will usually yellow in less than five years if not removed. Find a reputable retailer by searching online.

Have it made into a clutch purse
If you're not sentimental about preserving your gown, use the material to create something you can use again and again—a clutch purse. Find a talented seamstress who can create the bag for you and add embellishments and detailing.

Trash the Dress session
Hire your photographer for a post-wedding Trash the Dress photo session at the beach, a lake, a field, or an urban setting. A Trash the Dress shoot can involve both the bride and groom and is a time to be totally uninhibited, express yourselves and let loose. For many, the fun and often sexy photos are more of a keepsake than the gown.

Make it into handkerchiefs
Thank your loved ones for helping with your wedding day by creating a set of handkerchiefs out of your wedding gown. Handkerchiefs are easy to sew yourself, or have a tailor do it for you.

Let a family member use it to wrap her bouquet stem
A beautiful, personal touch is wrapping the stem of a wedding bouquet with a strip of fabric or lace from a relative's wedding gown. Give a swatch of your dress to each of your female family members to use for their wedding bouquets if they choose.

Make into a garter
A garter is a fairly simple sewing project that you can do using the fabric from your gown. Give the garters you make to friends who are getting married as their "something borrowed."

TOP 10 FUN WEDDING TRENDS

Chandeliers from trees
Rent or buy a few chandeliers to hang from trees around your ceremony or reception site. The

synergy of indoor lighting with an outdoor setting is breathtaking. Strings of white lights complement the chandeliers perfectly.

Candy buffet

Create a candy buffet to match your wedding colors and it can double as both décor and guests' favors. Choose several different types of candy, set out vellum bags and ties, and include metal scoops so guests can take home a sweet treat.

Custom cocktails

Serving a custom cocktail with beer and wine can not only save you money on bar costs, it tells your guests a story about you as a couple. Choose a drink that speaks to your heritage or that you enjoyed together on a special date. If there's a good story behind the libation, set out a card explaining the details on the bar for guests to read.

Fruits and vegetables in bouquets and centerpieces

Incorporating fruit and vegetables in your centerpieces and bouquets not only complements flowers beautifully but adds a modern, urban glamour to décor. Cut down on floral costs by including lemons, limes, kumquats, apples, artichokes, heirloom tomatoes, and more.

Mustaches or lips on a stick for photos

Wedding guests get silly for photos with a mustache on a stick, lips on a stick or any other funny prop you can come up with. They're an easy project you can make yourself, or order them online.

Photo booths

Even couples on a budget are saving their one splurge for a photo booth rental. A photo booth is a fun way to capture guests' candid moments and gives them a souvenir to take home from the wedding—the booth prints two sets of photo strips, one for the bride and groom and one for the guest.

Same day edit wedding video or slideshow

Many videographers are now offering day-of videos in which the footage shot at the ceremony is quickly edited during the cocktail hour and dinner and shown at the reception as a short video compilation or slideshow of stills. Always a fun surprise, you'll have guests and family laughing and crying all over again.

Birdcage to hold well wishes from guests

The classic guest book gets replaced with a whimsical twist. Purchase a rounded wire birdcage and have guests write their names and well wishes on cards that they drop into the cage. You might even consider a "love birds" theme.

Build a photo backdrop

Creative couples should consider making their own photo backdrop as a personalized and cost-effective alternative to a photo booth. Hang a large, colorful piece of fabric or printed wallpaper on a wooden backdrop and have guests pose in front of it. Set out empty frames or props for guests to use.

Antique typewriter guest book

Check online (eBay, Etsy, Craigslist, etc.) for vintage classic typewriters. A long scroll of paper threaded through the typewriter allows guests to type you thoughtful notes and well wishes throughout the day.

TOP 10 MOST AFFORDABLE HONEYMOON DESTINATIONS

* Mexico
* Las Vegas
* Florida
* Jamaica
* Dominican Republic
* Bahamas
* California
* Hawaii
* Canada
* Poconos

TOP 10 COOLEST VENUES

Lowndes Grove, Charleston, SC

A national historic landmark situated on 14 stunning river-side acres, Lowndes Grove is the last waterfront estate on the Charleston peninsula. The circa-1786 plantation home with two piazzas, a large lawn, multiple terraces, and beautiful oak trees and Spanish moss, makes for exquisite accommodations full of Southern charm for weddings of any size.
www.lowndesgrove.com

Tlaquepaque Arts & Crafts Village, Sedona, AZ

With a stunning backdrop of Sedona's famed Red Rocks, Tlaquepaque Village is a one-of-a-kind venue for an intimate wedding. Fashioned after a Mexican artisans' village, up to 100 guests can enjoy vine-covered adobe walls, cobblestone walkways, garden nooks, sweeping sycamore trees, bubbling fountains and glowing luminaries. Guests can watch you tie the knot at the quaint and beautiful chapel at Tlaquepaque.
www.tlaq.com

Atlanta History Center, Atlanta, GA

One of the most spectacular sites for a wedding, the Atlanta History Center is brimming with Southern charm, sprawling wooded gardens and historic buildings—it's no surprise that Margaret Mitchell

wrote *Gone with the Wind* here. With several lawns, gardens and ballrooms to choose from, this gorgeous historic venue can host events from 50 to 750 guests.
www.atlantahistorycenter.com

The Parker, Palm Springs, CA

The Parker Palm Springs has become known as a hip, fun location for weddings that don't take themselves too seriously. With beautiful lawns and gardens, hammocks, fire pits, croquet, an award-winning spa, and private villas, The Parker is a departure from the traditional ballroom wedding (although they can provide that, too). Their friendly staff can coordinate a complete weekend-long event for you and your guests.
www.theparkerpalmsprings.com

SmogShoppe, Culver City, CA

Once a 1980s smog-check center, SmogShoppe is now California's greenest (an LEED Platinum Candidate) event space. Fueled completely by solar power and featuring vertical gardens, desert plants, and chic vintage furnishings, SmogShoppe has quickly become one of the country's hottest wedding venues.
www.smogshoppe.com

Calamigos Ranch, Malibu, CA

Nestled against the breathtaking Malibu Mountains, this 130-acre expanse features the natural elegance of waterfalls, lakes and lush greenery. Elegantly appointed reception facilities adjoin each ceremony site with various indoor and outdoor locations to accommodate from 75 to 500 guests or more.
www.calamigos.com

Treehouse Point, Seattle, WA

Located 22 miles outside of Seattle, Treehouse Point is a charming, totally unique venue for an intimate wedding. Running streams and towering trees draped in lush moss surround cozy tree houses where the owners strive for sustainability and to support the community with local, organic food and original artwork.
www.treehousepoint.com

Auberge du Soleil, Napa Valley, CA

Terraced on a hillside overlooking Napa Valley's vineyards, Auberge du Soleil is one of wine country's most luxurious spots for a wedding. With private dining areas and decks for events, an acclaimed culinary team, and unparalleled views, up to 120 guests will be wowed by the experience.
www.aubergedusoleil.com

Barr Mansion, Austin, TX

This elegant 19th-century mansion is now the first and only Certified Organic events facility in the country. For the eco-friendly couple, Barr Mansion provides organic cotton, hemp, or recycled fabrics and a "zero-waste" facility in which all food goes to compost and back to the surrounding gardens.

Host a large or small wedding among the rose-filled gardens, tented lawns, beautiful pecan trees, or in the mansion's ballroom.
www.barrmansion.com

St. Bartholomew's Church, Manhattan, NY
For a Christian ceremony in New York City, famed St. Bartholomew's Church is unmatched in beauty and cultural and social significance. A beautiful 5,000-square-foot terrace overlooking Park Avenue, amazing catering, and a full event-planning team make this a coveted location for religious weddings.
www.stbarts.org

TOP 10 HONEYMOON DESTINATIONS

* Hawaii
* Mexico
* St. Lucia
* Fiji
* Las Vegas
* Italy
* Jamaica
* Virgin Islands
* African Safari
* Greek Isles

TOP 10 DESSERT ALTERNATIVES

Gourmet popcorn & pretzel bar
For a sweet and savory combo guests will love, create a gourmet popcorn and pretzel bar with caramel, melted chocolate, coconut, peanut butter, and more. Provide take-away bags and ties.

Gourmet donuts
Donuts may just be the new cupcakes when it comes to trendy wedding cake alternatives. Gourmet flavors, glazes and fillings mean endless options. Provide take-away boxes for guests to bring home extra donuts as favors. Plus, many gourmet donut bakers are happy to fill special requests, such as vegan donuts or donut towers.

Spiked sweets
Various types of alcohol, including brandy, rum, whiskey, Frangelico, and even beer, are showing up in cupcakes and cakes in a modern twist on classic desserts. Flavors might include mojito, piña colada, eggnog, or spiked apple cider. Just be sure to label the spiked sweets and provide guests with "virgin" options as well.

TOP 10 TRENDS, IDEAS & RESOURCES

Personalized chocolate treats

M&Ms, chocolate bars, chocolate coins and more can be personalized with your names, wedding date and colors. Choose a variety and set them out on a beautifully decorated table for guests to enjoy.

Cake pops

Cake pops are decadent little bites of cake on a stick, dipped in candy coating to resemble a colorful lollipop. You can try a variety of colors and flavors, and they're so easy to make, a few family members or friends could always pitch in to bake them for you!

French macarons

A classic French pastry similar to a meringue, macarons were traditionally given as favors in the past, but brides and grooms found the beautiful treats were upstaging their wedding cake! Have a French pastry chef create macarons in the colors and flavors you choose for a delicate, delicious and elegant dessert.

Mini fruit pies

For those non-chocolate lovers, mini fruit pies are a great alternative, especially for a rustic venue. Have your baker create several different seasonal flavors—from apple to peach to strawberry-rhubarb — so guests can try the lot.

Candy buffet

An extensive candy buffet means guests won't even miss wedding cake. Choose a wide variety of sweet, sour, nutty and chocolate-y candy in your wedding colors. Label each type and set out scoops and bags so guests can take an assortment.

Shot-glass desserts

Shot-glass desserts, such as chocolate cake, strawberry cheesecake or tiramisu, are the perfect contemporary alternative to wedding cake. These decadent mini desserts are a way for guests to try a variety of flavors in a modern way.

Cupcakes

Cupcake towers are popping up at weddings all over. At $3 or less each, cupcakes can save you money on a traditional wedding cake and mean you can have an assortment of flavors, colors and decorations for guests to try.

TOP 10 EVENT PLANNERS

Lisa Vorce, Oh, How Charming!

The mark of a Lisa Vorce wedding is that every last detail appears perfectly thought out, nothing overlooked. A boutique sensibility—smaller client list, greater attention to detail—means that Oh,

How Charming! Events are meticulously designed and executed, transporting guests to another world — a Moroccan spice market, a Balinese garden, a Maui beach, or a Tuscan farmhouse, for instance. http://ohhowcharming.com

Beth Helmstetter, Beth Helmstetter Events
Based in Los Angeles with a sister studio in Hawaii, this boutique-style company specializes in intimate events and destination weddings worldwide. An amazing sense of style, careful eye, business savvy, and discerning client list makes Helmstetter a much-sought-after planner in California and beyond. www.bethhelmstetter.com

Amy Mancuso, Amy Mancuso Events
Phoenix's Amy Mancuso studied under the legendary Colin Cowie and now plans both intimate and lavish affairs (she planned *Baywatch*'s Gena Lee Nolin's wedding in 2004). With more than 12 years of experience, she is a preferred vendor at most of the premier hotels and resorts in the Phoenix area. www.amymancuso.com

Jennifer Rose-Sandy, Salt Harbor Designs
Texas-based Salt Harbor Designs combines owner Jennifer Rose-Sandy's love of paper, flowers, fabric, lighting, and color to create an event aesthetic that is typically described as organic, natural and modern. www.saltharbor.com

Ann David and Nicky Reinhard, David Reinhard Events
Whether you're getting married in New York City, the Hamptons, or a destination wedding, the duo of planners behind this New York-based event planning company provides the utmost in personal attention to create high-end, sophisticated affairs. www.davidreinhard.com

Vanessa V. Vazquez, V3 Events
Serving Southern California and beyond, V3 Events offers an extensive range of services, from full planning assistance, to day-of coordination, to everything in between. Vanessa Vazquez's attentiveness and creativity will help you plan the wedding of your dreams down to the last detail. www.v3events.com

Heather Balliet, Amorology
In Heather Balliet's own words, "There may not be a science to love, but there is to planning the perfect wedding." Whether you choose à la carte services or full service creative design and planning, Amorology weddings are always full of color, texture and love. http://amorologyweddings.com

Pamela Barefoot, Atrendy Wedding
Atrendy Wedding owner, wedding planner Pamela Barefoot, blends modern trends with classic design when creating fabulous weddings for clients in D.C., Virginia and Maryland. Atrendy plans weddings

that are stylish, chic and glamorous, within a bride and groom's budget.
www.atrendywedding.com

Lara Casey, Bliss Event Group

Serving North Carolina, Florida, Alabama and Georgia, Lara Casey, also the publisher of *Southern Weddings Magazine*, is one of the most sought-after planners in the South. Bliss Event Group can handle all your wedding needs, including flowers, ceremony and reception locations, cake design, signature drink creation, linens, lighting, canopies, and more.
www.blisseventgroup.com

Lori Stephenson, LOLA Event Productions

Chicago-based LOLA Productions creates personalized, savvy events that harmonize every aspect, from the flowers to the food to the event flow. Better still, a portion of LOLA proceeds support several different charities.
www.lolaeventproductions.com

TOP 10 DESTINATION WEDDING LOCATIONS

* Mexico
* Hawaii
* Jamaica
* Las Vegas
* Florida
* Bahamas
* Caribbean
* Southern California
* Bermuda
* Napa Valley Wine Country

TOP 10 WAYS TO SAVE MONEY

Use non-floral elements instead of flowers

Flowers can add up quickly and cost thousands of dollars. To cut back, incorporate non-floral elements to complement or substitute for floral decorations.

Trim the guest list

If you're planning a bigger affair, an easy way to save is to pare down the guest list. Removing just 10 guests can save $100 a head many times, or $1,000.

Have a wedding brunch or cocktail and hors d'oeuvres wedding
People eat and drink much less at a brunch wedding than at night, saving you money on the bar tab and catering. A cocktail and hors d'oeuvres wedding where a formal dinner isn't served will save money on costly catering. Just be sure there is no mistake that a full meal won't be served.

Wear a dress that's not a "wedding dress"
Look for dresses from designers such as BCBG, Nicole Miller, Vera Wang, or ABS, in their non-wedding lines. You will often find gorgeous gowns with beautiful detailing, lace, and beading that are less than $500 simply because they aren't technically considered "wedding" gowns.

Ask friends and family pitch in
Ask a few people who can bake to make cupcakes or cakes—you'll save money and have a variety of treats. Or, enlist a friend who can sew to make your ring pillow or personalize table linens, for instance. Have the groom and his buddies pitch in to build the wedding arch or make place card holders. This will help make your wedding really personal, as well as cut costs.

Get married on a Friday or Sunday
Reception venues are always less expensive when you book a day other than Saturday night. Another plus is that Saturdays book up quickly, so you will have a broader choice of dates when you go with a Friday or Sunday.

Focus on the one or two most memorable and important details only
Will your guests remember your monogrammed napkins? If your invitation had a tri-fold and inner envelope? Probably not. But they will remember if you included special details, such as having a fun photo booth or a great live band that kept them dancing all night.

Hire a photographer only for your ceremony and have guests take candids at the reception
Some of the most important photos from your wedding day are those from the ceremony, and some of the most fun photos are the candids from the reception. Photography can put a big dent in a small budget, so save money by hiring a professional only for the ceremony and ask friends and family to take lots of photos at the reception. Then create a Flickr or Photobucket account, give everyone the password, and have them upload the pictures for all to share.

Serve a custom cocktail with beer and wine
Have beer and wine, but also have a personal drink. Give away the recipe for your personalized drink, as well as a special glass to drink it in.

Skip favors
Unless they're immediately edible, many guests will leave favors behind. Pass on candles, mini photo frames, CDs and more and save hundreds of dollars.

TOP 10 UP-AND-COMING GOWN DESIGNERS

Ida Sjöstedt

Stockholm-born designer Ida Sjöstedt creates beautiful, ethereal gowns with vintage 1970s appeal. She likes to say she creates gowns for women who don't take dressing up too seriously and who see wedding fashion as fun.
www.idasjostedt.com

Melissa Blackburn

Gown designer Melissa Blackburn, based in Provo, Utah, believes a bride should be ecstatic about her gown. Her motto is: "I will not rest until the gown exceeds expectations and all details are perfect," and she delivers no less than impeccable handcrafted work.
www.melissablackburn.net

Maria Lucia Hohan

Feminine, whimsical, ethereal, playful, and confident—these are all words to describe the one-of-a-kind gowns by Maria Lucia Hohan. With unique detailing and in a range of hues for the traditional and nontraditional bride alike, these well-priced gowns are gorgeous standouts.
http://www.marialuciahohan.com/

Sarah Seven

With a deep desire for the romance and simple decadence of a bygone era of femininity, Portland designer, Sarah Seven, creates unique bridal gowns that are vintage-inspired but decidedly modern. Her bridal collection includes intricate arrangements of blossoming ruffles, delicate fabrics, and flowing layers made of silk, wool, linen, cotton voile, as well as recycled vintage fabrics.
www.sarahseven.com

Elizabeth Dye

Portland-based Elizabeth Dye takes inspiration from the past, often using rare fabrics and one-of-a-kind details in her modern-romantic pieces. Dye's streamlined silhouettes have a graceful and feminine appeal.
www.elizabethdye.com

Natural Bridal Collection

Designer Morgan Boszilkov believes in creating exceptionally designed gowns that are eco-friendly without sacrificing luxury, style, or beauty. Natural Bridal Collection gowns are hand-crafted using sustainable fabrics, striving to apply green and socially responsible principles. In addition, 5% of profits are donated to environmental causes.
www.naturalbridals.com

Joan Shum

Joan Shum's truly unique bridal collection unites a passion for art, costume and fashion into a line of

elegant gowns. Her celebrated corset bridal line consists only of corsets and skirts, which allow brides to create their own sense of style.
http://www.etsy.com/shop/joanshum

Carol Hannah

Project Runway runner-up Carol Hannah's debut wedding collection could be described as "a modern day fairy at a cocktail party." Her design aesthetic combines whimsy with organic details including raw edges and fabric handwork.
www.etsy.com/shop/theweddingcollection

Angelo Lambrou

Angelo Lambrou creates gowns in Old World style, reminiscent of high fashion in Milan, London, or Paris. His gowns are infused with color and glamour, for the bride who wishes to stand out among the crowd.
www.angelolambrou.com

Deborah Lindquist

Lindquist's eco-chic wedding collection has met rave reviews since its inception. The collection is bursting with couture-inspired gowns, chic column skirts, bustier tops, and cashmere shrugs and sweaters.
www.deborahlindquist.com

TOP 10 WEDDING MOVIES

* *The Wedding Singer*
* *Father of the Bride*
* *My Best Friend's Wedding*
* *My Big Fat Greek Wedding*
* *Wedding Crashers*
* *Bridesmaids*
* *The Wedding Planner*
* *Mama Mia*
* *Muriel's Wedding*
* *Four Weddings and A Funeral*

TOP 10 UNIQUE RECEPTION IDEAS

Day-of wedding video at the reception

Guests will be surprised and delighted by a day-of wedding video shown during the reception. Have your videographer work during the cocktail hour and meal to create a several-minute-long video compilation of the day's prior highlights, such as the bride and groom getting ready, the ceremony, and the first look.

Barn hoedown

Consider a barn as your reception venue—with great lighting and music, it becomes a cozy, homey atmosphere. Arrange an outdoor firepit with s'mores, serve cold beer, and put out hay bales covered with colorful blankets as seats. Hire a live bluegrass band to have guests dancing all night long.

Lawn games

Croquet, horseshoes and badminton, on your wedding day? Yes! Guests can enjoy the sunshine while playing a few rounds with the bride and groom. And because lawn games are low-key, the bride won't feel restricted by her gown. Plus, the photos will be fabulous, fun and memorable.

Wine tasting reception

Have a local winery or restaurant create a fun wine tasting experience for you and your guests at your reception. Wines can be paired with food so guests also get a complete meal. Wine tasting is an amazing way to get guests chatting and meeting one another.

Clambake

A classic East Coast-style clambake is a lively, laid-back way to celebrate good food, weather, and friends and family. The hands-on nature of the clambake makes it a great way for guests to mingle. Don't forget warm blankets and a fire for guests to stay warm at this outdoor event.

Backyard barbecue

A formal dinner in a large ballroom may not be the best way to mingle with guests. Hire a caterer who specializes in gourmet comfort food to create a backyard barbecue-themed reception. Guests will feel relaxed and comfortable and can enjoy delicious dinner fare.

Kissing booth

Take a modern, fun twist on the traditional receiving line by creating a kissing booth. The bride and groom give handshakes, hugs or kisses on the cheek to every guest who comes through the booth. Later, leave the kissing booth open for guests to step in and pucker up while your photographer captures each moment.

Aquarium reception

The low light of an aquarium creates a romantic vibe for a reception dinner. Imagine dining with your guests while graceful, elegant fish swim past in the background! Find an aquarium in your area that caters to weddings.

Family style dinner and chalkboard menu

Family style dining at a wedding is a wonderful spin on the buffet line. Each table gets a plate of each course to share, which also creates fun interaction between guests. As guests enter the reception dining area, set out a large chalkboard menu with the "daily specials," as a café would.

Zoo reception
The zoo is a fun and totally unique place to get married. Guests of all ages will love the sights and sounds, and many zoos provide complete event-planning services as well.

TOP 10 NON-FLORAL DÉCOR ELEMENTS

Topiaries
Rent miniature potted topiaries from a local florist for a whimsical look that doesn't cost a fortune, and use them to line aisles or serve as centerpieces. Tying on ribbon in your wedding colors gives them a personalized look.

Beachgrass
Beachgrass lends a Martha's Vineyard-esque feel when used in bouquets, aisle decorations, centerpieces and more. Carry the beachgrass design through your invitation suite as well. Beachgrass blends well with flowers or makes a modern statement when grouped alone in tall vases.

Kumquats
Tiny orange kumquats are showing up in bouquets and centerpieces because of their bright color and fresh citrus scent, which make a great complement to flowers. Kumquats are in season in late-winter, spring and early summer.

Wine corks
Wine corks make a simple, inexpensive, and versatile bit of décor. Fill vases or mason jars with them for a vineyard-themed wedding. To act as seating card holders, cut vertical slits in the corks to hold cards in place. You can even order personalized wine corks online at sites like Etsy.com.

Succulents
Succulents make a hardy, less expensive alternative to flowers in bouquets and centerpieces. Use individual potted succulents as favors that will live much longer than traditional blooms. Find succulents at your local nursery and buy them in bulk to cut costs.

Feathers
Feathers make beautiful décor because they can be dyed or bleached and clustered alone or combined with flowers to create a glamorous, dramatic look. From peacock feathers to guinea feathers, this is non-floral trend that is popping up in bouquets, hairpieces, tablescapes and more.

Tree trunk sections
Get a rustic feel by using horizontal sections of real trees as the base for your cake and centerpieces

and as place card holders.

Terrariums

Terrariums can be purchased or make a cool DIY project for creative brides. Plant moss, succulents, tiny flowers and plants, and stones in apothecary jars, fishbowls, mason jars or vases to give wedding tables a modern, organic feel your guests will love investigating.

Strands of crystals

Weddings are getting a little (or a lot) of bling thanks to the crystal strands that are showing up hanging from trees, chandeliers, and centerpieces. Let crystal décor echo the shine and glamour of an upscale, sophisticated ceremony.

Artichokes

Artichokes come in a range of sizes and colors—large to mini in purple, green and even white—and have petal-like leaves that complement flowers beautifully. Use them as place card holders, in centerpieces, and as décor on the buffet table.

TOP 100 FAQs

Karen French

KAREN FRENCH

TIFFANY & CO.

TIFFANY & CO.

KAREN FRENCH

Sung
and
Elisa
4/26/08

KAREN FRENCH

KAREN FRENCH

KAREN FRENCH

TOP 100 FAQS

FINDING THE PERSON YOU LOVE, MAKING PLANS to the spend the rest of your lives together, creating your perfect wedding day—about 5 million people each year tie the knot, and they are asking the same questions when it comes to wedding planning.

WedSpace.com contains full answers to more than 1,000 commonly asked wedding and honeymoon questions, compiled from the thousands of couples registered on the site. Engaged couples everywhere know they can come to WedSpace.com with their most pressing wedding questions and get answers from the top wedding experts and professionals in the country.

From WedSpace.com's extensive forums, this chapter lists the top 100 most frequently asked wedding questions. This section explores every important topic in wedding and honeymoon planning, from budgeting, to bridal fashion and beauty, to choosing a ceremony and reception site, to saving money with your wedding vendors.

If you have a wedding or honeymoon planning question you don't see on this list, log on to WedSpace.com and search among thousands of questions in our Q&A/Forums section. If you still don't find what you're looking for, ask your question on our forum to get answers from wedding professionals and other couples just like you.

WedSpace.com can help you every step of the way as you plan one of the most important days of your life—your wedding day!

1. **What is the first thing a couple should do to start planning the wedding?**
The first thing a couple should do is sit down and have an open and honest conversation about what type of wedding they would like to have, how much money they would like to spend, who is going to pay for what, and any other priorities they have for the wedding.

2. **How do I determine the total cost of my wedding?**
Start with the amount of money you would like to spend on your wedding. Now, estimate how much money you will spend on certain parts of or items in the wedding, such as your dress, the food and beverages, the music, etc. Add these amounts together. That subtotal is your projected wedding budget. As you go, you should record how much you actually end up spending on these items. This will help you stay within your budget.

3. **What is the average cost of a wedding in the U.S.?**
The average U.S. wedding costs slightly more than $21,000.

4. **How should my wedding budget break down?**
Here is how an average wedding budget typically breaks down for each aspect. Naturally, you may choose to splurge or save in certain areas, so this breakdown can be adjusted as need be.

> Ceremony = 5% of Budget
> Wedding Attire = 10% of Budget
> Photography = 9% of Budget
> Videography = 5% of Budget
> Stationery = 4% of Budget
> Reception = 35% of Budget
> Music = 5% of Budget
> Flowers = 6% of Budget
> Decorations = 3% of Budget
> Transportation = 2% of Budget
> Rental Items = 3% of Budget
> Gifts = 3% of Budget
> Miscellaneous (Marriage license, taxes, etc.) = 4% of Budget

5. **How many couples pay for their own weddings?**
With couples getting married later in life than decades past, more and more people are paying for their own weddings. A recent survey showed that 30 percent of couples are paying for all or part of their weddings.

6. **What are the benefits of creating a wedding website?**
Building a wedding website gives your guests a place to go to see all the details of your wedding, from your proposal story to the members of the wedding party to your registry to the details of the "what, where, when" of the wedding day.

7. How can we tell our guests about our wedding website?

You can include the URL in your Save the Date cards or on your invitations and tell your guests to visit your site for complete details of the wedding. Just remember that some older people, like grandparents, may not be Internet-savvy, so you may still want to include maps and such with your invitations.

8. Should I hire a wedding consultant?

Strongly consider engaging the services of a wedding consultant. Contrary to what many people believe, a wedding consultant is part of your wedding budget, not an extra expense! A good wedding consultant should be able to save you at least the amount of his or her fee by suggesting less expensive alternatives that still enhance your wedding. In addition, many consultants obtain discounts from the service providers they work with. If this is not enough, they are more than worth their fee by serving as an intermediary between you and your parents and/or service providers. When hiring a wedding consultant, make sure you check his or her references. Ask the consultant if he or she is a member of the Association of Bridal Consultants (ABC) and ask to see a current membership certificate. All ABC members agree to uphold a Code of Ethics and Standards of Membership.

9. What is a wedding designer? Is this different from my wedding consultant?

They actually serve much of the same purpose—both are types of event planners who will help you create the wedding of your dreams. The difference is a wedding designer is usually a person with specific formal training and experience in floral arrangements, interior design, or even fashion who can help you create an overarching theme or "brand" for your wedding that flows through every aspect, from the invitations to the centerpieces. This person gives you creative ideas that you can use to lend a cohesive theme to your wedding.

10. Do I need to invite my wedding planner to parties like the bridal shower, etc?

You are not obligated to invite your wedding planner, unless you choose to.

11. How much does a wedding consultant cost?

Wedding consultants can cost from $500 to $10,000. It depends who you hire and for how long, and also if they charge hourly or set a flat rate. Some people hire a consultant for the entire wedding planning process and some hire one only for the Big Day.

12. Should I plan to incorporate do-it-yourself projects in my wedding planning?

DIY wedding projects can save money at times and may give your wedding a personal touch, but they can also become stressful for the couple. A good tip is to look online at different design sites and wedding blogs and find DIY projects that brides have posted. Brides will post materials to buy, cost, and the timeline for the projects. That way you can get a feel for how long a project will take and how labor-intensive it will be.

13. **What should I consider when looking at or booking a ceremony site?**

Your selection of a ceremony site will be influenced by the formality of your wedding, the season, the number of guests expected and your religious affiliation. Consider issues such as proximity of the ceremony site to the reception site, parking availability, handicapped accessibility, and time constraints.

14. **If we want a beach wedding, do we need a permit?**

Yes, you should contact the city hall of the area and find out what permits you need to attain and how much they cost.

15. **If we have our ceremony in a park, what do we need to consider?**

You should consider that you will need to obtain the correct permits from the city, as well as rent everything your guests need to be comfortable. This includes chairs and extras like portable bathrooms.

16. **What should we consider if we are going to do a dove release after being pronounced husband and wife?**

You should find a reputable company in your area that will handle the dove release in an ethical way. This means not releasing doves at night, in bad weather, inside a building, or beyond where they can easily fly back.

17. **What should we know if we are considering a butterfly release?**

You should find a company that specializes in butterfly releases for weddings. The butterflies will arrive in a package with instructions about how to keep them dormant until the wedding. You should only release butterflies when it is a clear day, not at night or in inclement weather. Many times, butterflies will land on your dress or bouquet!

18. **How can we honor a loved one who has passed away during our ceremony?**

Ultimately, how you choose to honor a lost loved one is up to you and your fiancé; however you might consider keeping a seat at the ceremony empty and placing a flower or photo on the chair. You might also ask the officiant to say a prayer for that person or mention him or her during the ceremony.

19. **Who can officiate my wedding?**

Here are some of the options you have when considering who to officiate your wedding: a priest, clergyman, minister, pastor, chaplain, Rabbi, judge, or Justice of the Peace.

20. **Can we have a friend or family member preside over our ceremony?**

It is becoming increasingly popular to have a friend or loved one become ordained and act as your officiant. Make sure this person goes through an accredited program or online program, and double-check that it will be legal.

21.   How much is the officiant's gratuity?
The officiant's gratuity is usually $50 to $250.

22.   Should I include my officiant on my guest list?
Your officiant and his or her partner should be invited to your reception, so don't forget to include them on your guest list and seating chart.

23.   How can I personalize my marriage vows?
As with all your ceremony plans, be sure to discuss your ideas for marriage vows with your officiant. The following are some ideas that you might want to consider when planning your marriage vows:

- You and your fiancé could write your own personal marriage vows and keep them secret from one another until the actual ceremony.
- Incorporate your guests and family members into your vows by acknowledging their presence at the ceremony.
- Describe what you cherish most about your partner and what you hope for your future together.
- Describe your commitment to and love for one another.
- Discuss your feelings and beliefs about marriage.
- If either of you has children from a previous marriage, mention these children in your vows and discuss your mutual love for and commitment to them.

24.   When should I play music at my ceremony?
Ceremony music is the music played during the ceremony; i.e., prelude, processional, ceremony, recessional and postlude. Prelude music is played 15 to 30 minutes before the ceremony begins and while guests are being seated. Processional music is played as the wedding party enters the ceremony site. Ceremony music is played during the ceremony. Recessional music is played as the wedding party leaves the ceremony site. Postlude music is played while the guests leave the ceremony site.

25.   How can I save money on ceremony music?
Hire student musicians from your local university or high school. Ask a friend to sing or play at your ceremony; they will be honored. If you're planning to hire a band for your reception, consider hiring a scaled-down version of the same band to play at your ceremony, such as a trio of flute, guitar, and vocals. This could enable you to negotiate a "package" price. If you're planning to hire a DJ for your reception, consider hiring him or her to play pre-recorded music at your ceremony.

26.   What is the price range of wedding dresses?
Wedding dresses can range anywhere from $300 to $10,000, depending on the designer, detailing and material.

27. How many dress fittings do I need to have?

You should have at least 3 fittings. The first fitting should be 6 months before, the second fitting should be 1 month before, and the final fitting is about 1 week before.

28. What is a fingertip veil?

This is the most common veil length, reaching to the fingertips. It can be worn with a variety of dress styles.

29. What is a birdcage veil?

A vintage look, a birdcage veil is made of lace or French netting that covers the face.

30. What is a mantilla veil?

A mantilla veil is a Spanish-inspired veil that drapes over the head and is usually made of lace.

31. What is a chapel veil?

A chapel veil is a formal look, extending 2½ yards from the headpiece, flowing down over the train of the dress.

32. What is a cathedral veil?

The most formal veil, a cathedral extends 3½ yards from the headpiece.

33. What should I consider if I want to wear fresh flowers in my hair?

Choose a hardy bloom like daisies or roses. Delicate flowers like sweet peas and tulips will wilt quickly. Another popular flower to wear in the hair is the gardenia, which has a soft, pretty scent.

34. Should I have my hair or makeup done first on my wedding day?

You should always have your hair done first.

35. What kind of makeup should I avoid on my wedding day?

Beware of using too much shimmer or glitter, as these types of makeup will cause you to appear shiny in your pictures. A light shimmer used to highlight certain areas such as your cheekbones and brow bones is OK, but you may want to take test photos before the wedding day to see how it is going to look. It is best to use a waterproof mascara and eyeliner, especially if you know you will be shedding a few tears on your big day. Finally, don't wear a ton of makeup if you don't normally. You want to look like yourself!

36. My makeup artist suggested airbrush makeup. What is airbrush makeup?

Airbrush makeup is foundation that is applied with a spray tool that gives even, all-over coverage that won't streak, run, or fade during the day. Thus, it is a top choice for bridal makeup. It also provides beautiful coverage for photos.

37.   **What do diamonds symbolize?**
Throughout the world, diamonds are used to symbolize love and the unbreakable bond of marriage.

38.   **What is the average size of the diamond engagement ring today?**
Today, the average size of the diamond on an engagement ring is about .75 carats.

39.   **What should we consider when deciding what style of wedding bands to get?**
The bride's wedding band should complement her engagement ring in style and metal. For the groom, consider his lifestyle when choosing a wedding band. Certain metals are stronger and will resist wear and tear better than others. For instance, if you work with your hands and will be wearing your wedding band every day, you will want to avoid any soft metals. A durable metal, like titanium, is a good choice. Platinum is the most expensive metal for a ring. Palladium is an alternative to platinum that is less expensive. White gold also looks similar to platinum, but costs about half as much. You might also talk to a jeweler about yellow gold, rose gold, and other unique metal options.

40.   **What does the term "color" mean in terms of a diamond?**
A diamond's color scale ranges from D to Z. Keep in mind that the slight color of near colorless diamonds is usually visible only through a magnifying lens and from the underside of the diamond. Therefore, minor shades of color, are hard to see in mounted stones.

    D to F: Colorless
    G to J: Near colorless
    K to M: Faint yellow
    N to R: Very light yellow
    S to Z: Light yellow
    Z+: Fancy or colored

41.   **What should I get in writing before I buy a diamond?**
Before you purchase a diamond, make sure you get a detailed appraisal of the diamond in writing. Also get in writing any other policy such as money-back or trade-in as well as whether the purchase is subject to verification of GIA certification.

42.   **When should the groom reserve tuxedos or suits?**
Reserve tuxedos for yourself and your ushers several weeks before the wedding to ensure a wide selection and to allow enough time for alterations. Plan to pick up the tuxedos a few days before the wedding to allow time for last minute alterations in case they don't fit properly. Ask about the store's return policy and be sure you delegate to the appropriate person (usually your best man) the responsibility of returning all tuxedos within the time allotted. Ushers customarily pay for their own tuxedos.

43. What should I do about tux rentals if I have ushers who live out of the state or country?

Out-of-town men in your wedding party can be sized at any tuxedo shop. They can send their measurements to you or directly to the shop where you are going to rent your tuxedos. Make sure one of their first stops when they get to town for the wedding is the tux shop to try on their tuxedos and make sure there are no last-minute alterations needed.

44. Can I have my pet in the wedding?

Pets can absolutely participate in the wedding ceremony if your venue allows it. Many retailers sell mini tuxedos, ring pillows, and special wedding attire for pets. If the venue gives you the OK, ask a responsible family member or friend to be in charge of your pet. You don't want to have to worry in the event that the animal acts up, needs water, or has to relieve itself.

45. Do my bridesmaids have to wear matching dresses?

One dress may not look good on every woman in your wedding party. If you want, you can give your bridesmaids two or three styles from the same designer and let them choose the style they like best. Or, you can choose a specific color and let the ladies pick their own dresses. You may want to approve the dresses to be sure they coordinate and are of your liking.

46. What are the maid of honor's responsibilities?

- Helps bride select attire and address invitations.
- Plans bridal shower.
- Arrives at dressing site 2 hours before ceremony to assist bride in dressing.
- Arrives dressed at ceremony site 1 hour before the wedding for photographs.
- Arranges the bride's veil and train before the processional and recessional.
- Holds bride's bouquet and groom's ring, if no ring bearer, during the ceremony.
- Witnesses the signing of the marriage license.
- Keeps bride on schedule.
- Dances with best man during the bridal party dance.
- Helps bride change into her going away clothes.
- Mails wedding announcements after the wedding.
- Returns bridal slip, if rented.

47. What are the best man's responsibilities?

- Responsible for organizing ushers' activities.
- Organizes bachelor party for groom.
- Drives groom to ceremony site and sees that he is properly dressed before the wedding.

- Arrives dressed at ceremony site 1 hour before the wedding for photographs.
- Brings marriage license to wedding.
- Pays the clergyman, musicians, photographer, and any other service providers the day of the wedding.
- Holds the bride's ring for the groom, if no ring bearer, until needed by officiant.
- Witnesses the signing of the marriage license.
- Drives newlyweds to reception if no hired driver.
- Offers first toast at reception, usually before dinner.
- Keeps groom on schedule.
- Dances with maid of honor during the bridal party dance.
- May drive couple to airport or honeymoon suite.
- Oversees return of tuxedo rentals for groom and ushers, on time and in good condition.

48. What are the bridesmaids' responsibilities?
- Assist maid of honor in planning bridal shower.
- Assist bride with errands and addressing invitations.
- Participate in all pre-wedding parties.
- Arrive at dressing site 2 hours before ceremony.
- Arrive dressed at ceremony site 1 hour before the wedding for photographs.
- Walk behind ushers in order of height during the processional, either in pairs or in single file.
- Sit next to ushers at the head table.
- Dance with ushers and other important guests.
- Encourage single women to participate in the bouquet-tossing ceremony.

49. What are the ushers' responsibilities?
- Help best man with bachelor party.
- Arrive dressed at ceremony site one hour before the wedding for photographs.
- Distribute wedding programs and maps to the reception as guests arrive.
- Seat guests at the ceremony as follows:
  - If female, offer the right arm.
  - If male, walk along his left side.
  - If couple, offer right arm to female; male follows a step or two behind.
- Seat bride's guests in left pews.

· Seat groom's guests in right pews.
· Maintain equal number of guests in left and right pews, if possible.
· If a group of guests arrive at the same time, seat the eldest woman first.
· Just prior to the processional, escort groom's mother to her seat; then escort bride's mother to her seat.
· Two ushers may roll carpet down the aisle after both mothers are seated.
· If pew ribbons are used, two ushers may loosen them one row at a time after the ceremony.
· Direct guests to the reception site.
· Dance with bridesmaids and other important guests.

50. What are the mother of the bride's responsibilities?
· Helps prepare guest list for bride and her family.
· Helps plan the wedding ceremony and reception.
· Helps bride select her bridal gown.
· Helps bride keep track of gifts received.
· Selects her own attire according to the formality and color of the wedding.
· Makes accommodations for bride's out of town guests.
· Arrives dressed at ceremony site one hour before the wedding for photographs.
· Is the last person to be seated right before the processional begins.
· Sits in the left front pew to the left of bride's father during the ceremony.
· May stand up to signal the start of the processional.
· Can witness the signing of the marriage license.
· Dances with the groom after the first dance.
· Acts as hostess at the reception.

51. What are the father of the bride's responsibilities?
· Helps prepare guest list for bride and her family.
· Selects attire that complements groom's attire.
· Rides to the ceremony with bride in limousine.
· Arrives dressed at ceremony site one hour before the wedding for photographs.
· After giving bride away, sits in the left front pew to the right of bride's mother.
· If divorced, sits in second or third row unless financing

the wedding.
- When officiant asks, "Who gives this bride away?" answers, "Her mother and I do," or something similar.
- Can witness the signing of the marriage license.
- Dances with bride after first dance.
- Acts as host at the reception.

52. What are the mother of the groom's responsibilities?
- Helps prepare guest list for groom and his family.
- Selects attire that complements mother of the bride's attire.
- Makes accommodations for groom's out-of-town guests.
- With groom's father, plans rehearsal dinner.
- Arrives dressed at ceremony site one hour before the wedding for photographs.
- May stand up to signal the start of the processional.
- Can witness the signing of the marriage license.

53. What are the father of the groom's responsibilities?
- Helps prepare guest list for groom and his family.
- Selects attire that complements groom's attire.
- With groom's mother, plans rehearsal dinner.
- Offers toast to bride at rehearsal dinner.
- Arrives dressed at ceremony site one hour before the wedding for photographs.
- Can witness the signing of the marriage license.

54. What can I do if one of our parents wants to help plan the wedding?

It is not uncommon for parents to feel starved for attention during wedding planning. The mother of the bride will especially want to feel she is included. An easy way to include her in wedding planning is to put her in charge of invitations and RSVPs. She can address and send out invitations and keep track of who RSVPs—all important tasks. If you want, you can also invite her along to look at ceremony and reception sites or to meet vendors—just be clear with vendors that you are the point of contact, and be clear with her that you value her opinion, but the decisions are ultimately yours.

55. How much do photographers cost?

It depends upon the quality of the photographer and whether or not they charge a flat or hourly rate, but photographers' packages can range from $900 to $7,000. This is not an area in which you want to skimp, so if you have the budget for it, hire the best photographer you can.

56. Should I have my photographer shoot in black and white or color or a combination of both?

Black and white photography can be very dramatic and beautiful; however, the colorful aspects of your wedding, including your flowers, dresses, venue, and décor, won't be aptly captured. You should ask for a combination of black and white and color photos to capture the complete essence and ambience of your wedding.

57. What is the benefit of digital film?

Today, most photographers use digital format cameras. This can be great, because it makes it easy to switch between black and white and color without having to replace rolls of film or use multiple cameras. You will also probably get a lot more images to choose from, as photographers using a digital camera can shoot far more pictures. In addition, you can often purchase the files and print the photos you'd like yourself.

58. What should I consider when taking my engagement photos?

Decide whether you want candid shots, posed portrait shots, or a combination of both. Many couples prefer to have engagement photos taken outside and not in a studio; ask your photographer if he or she can scout locations. Engagement shoots can include more than one wardrobe change; bring outfits with bright colors and do not wear busy patterns or white, which do not photograph as nicely. Ask your photographer to take some classic bridal portraits (shots of just bride).

59. What percentage of my guest list can I expect to say they can attend?

For a traditional (non-destination) wedding, if you invite over 200 guests, estimate that about 25 percent of your guests will be unable to attend. If you are inviting fewer than 200 guests, consider that 15 to 20 percent will RSVP that they are unable to attend. However, you should always plan for every person on your list to RSVP "yes," to be on the safe side.

60. How many invitations should I order?

Order approximately 20 percent more stationery than your actual guest count. Allow a minimum of two weeks to address and mail the invitations, longer if using a calligrapher or if your guest list is very large. You may also want to consider ordering invitations to the rehearsal dinner, as these should be in the same style as the wedding invitation.

61. When should we mail our save the date cards?

Four to six months before the wedding.

62. When should we mail invitations?

Six to eight weeks before the wedding.

63. Should I have a candy buffet at my reception?

You can make a lovely candy buffet that acts as both décor and favors by arranging glass vases, bowls, and jars with various types of treats. Provide small boxes or vellum or clear bags so guests can take home a sample of candy. Select 5 to 10 kinds of candy. Get several pounds of each or one-quarter to one-half a pound of candy per person at your wedding.

64. How can I save money on my reception?

Reception sites that charge a room rental fee may waive this fee if you meet minimum requirements on food and beverages consumed. Try to negotiate this before you book the facility. Consider a brunch or early afternoon wedding so the reception will fall between meals, allowing you to serve hors d'oeuvres instead of a full meal. Consider serving hors d'oeuvres "buffet style." Your guests will eat less this way than if waiters and waitresses are constantly serving them hors d'oeuvres. Or tray-pass hors d'oeuvres during cocktail hour and choose a lighter meal. Compare two or three caterers; there is a wide price range between caterers for the same food. Compare the total cost of catering (main entrée plus hors d'oeuvres) when selecting a caterer.

65. What is the proper formation for the receiving line?

From left to right, this is the traditional order people stand in the receiving line:
- Bride's Mother
- Bride's Father
- Groom's Mother
- Groom's Father
- Bride
- Groom
- Maid of Honor
- Bridesmaids

66. What is the proper seating for the head table at the reception?

From left to right, this is the proper seating formation for the head table, if you have one at your reception:
- Bridesmaid
- Usher
- Bridesmaid
- Best Man
- Bride
- Groom
- Maid of Honor
- Usher
- Bridesmaid
- Usher

67. What is the proper seating for the parents' table at the reception?

The proper seating formation for the parents' table at the reception is as follows (assuming the table is round):

· Officiant
· Groom's Mother
· Groom's Father
· Bride's Mother
· Bride's Father
· Other Relatives

68. When should the toasting begin at the reception?

The toast begins after the receiving line breaks up at a cocktail reception or before dinner during a dinner reception. Toasts can also be offered after the main course or after the cake is served.

69. How do we select our catering menu?

The menu will be determined by your tastes and the season. Let the caterer know what type of cuisine and dishes you have in mind. You can also ask your caterer what his or her specialties are, and you may want to include those. If your reception is going to be at a hotel, restaurant or other facility that provides food, you will need to select a meal to serve your guests. Most of these facilities will have a predetermined menu from which to select your meal. Generally, you will want to serve a red meat option, a white meat or fish options, and a vegetarian option for your main course.

70. Should I provide meals for my vendors?

It is considered a courtesy to feed your photographer, videographer, and all other "service providers" at the reception. Check options and prices with your caterer or reception site manager. Make sure you allocate a place for your service providers to eat. You may want them to eat with your guests, or you may prefer setting a place outside the main room for them to eat. Your service providers may be more comfortable with the latter. You don't need to feed your service providers the same meal as your guests. You can order sandwiches or another less expensive meal for them. If the meal is a buffet, there should be enough food left after all your guests have been served for your service providers to eat. Tell them they are welcome to eat after all your guests have been served.

71. How can I figure out how much alcohol I need?

On average, you should allow one drink per person per hour at the reception. A bottle of champagne will usually serve six glasses. If you're hosting an open bar at a hotel or restaurant, ask the catering manager how they charge for liquor: by consumption or by number of bottles opened. Get this in writing, and then ask for a full consumption report after the event.

72. How much should I spend on alcohol?

Beverages at your reception can range anywhere from $8 to $35 per person, depending on the beverages and brands you choose to serve and the type of bar you choose.

73. How can I save money on the bar?
To keep beverage costs down, serve punch, wine, or nonalcoholic drinks only. If your caterer allows it, consider buying liquor from a wholesaler who will let you return unopened bottles. Or host beer, wine, and soft drinks only and have mixed drinks available on a cash basis. The bartending fee is often waived if you meet the minimum requirements on beverages consumed. Omit waiters and waitresses. People tend to drink almost twice as much if there are waiters and waitresses constantly asking them if they would like another drink, and then bringing drinks to them.

74. What are the different parts of the reception that I can select specific music for?
· Cocktail hour
· Newlyweds' entrance/Receiving line
· During dinner
· Toasts
· First dance
· Family dances
· Bouquet toss
· Garter removal and toss
· Cake cutting
· Money dance
· Ethnic dances
· Last dance

75. What should I consider when hiring a DJ to play music at my reception?
A great DJ can make a party, just as a below-average one can ruin it, so it is important that you choose carefully. The key to finding a good DJ is to find an experienced professional with an extensive song list. While DJs don't have demo tapes, many will provide a video that will give you an idea of their style. Along with the DJ's personal style, you will want to evaluate their playlist. Look for a wide variety of music, from different genres, as well as different eras. Inquire into the DJ's level of commitment; is the DJ doing this to earn extra money on the weekends or are weddings the DJ's primary business? A higher level of commitment often means a higher level of professionalism, as the DJ relies on referrals.

76. What leg does the bride wear the garter on?
You can wear the garter on either leg. Just wear it above the knee.

77. How much wedding cake should I order?
Talk to your baker about how much cake to order; you may only need to order cake for 75 percent of your RSVP list to avoid waste, for instance.

78. When during the reception should we cut the cake?
The cake cutting and photos come toward the end of the reception, following the bouquet toss and garter toss.

79. How much does a wedding cake cost?
It depends upon the bakery and the size of your cake, but they can range from $2 to $12 a piece.

80. When should I make my final floral selections?
Two to six weeks before the wedding.

81. How much does the bridal bouquet cost?
It can range from $75 to $500, depending on the type and quantity of flowers you use.

82. How much do bridesmaids' bouquets usually cost?
Depending on the type of flowers used and the sizes of the bouquets, bridesmaids' bouquets can cost from $25 to $100 each.

83. What are alternatives to throwing rose petals or rice as the bride and groom leave the reception?
Keep in mind that rose petals can stain carpets; rice can sting faces and make stairs dangerously slippery; and confetti is messy and hard to clean. An environmentally correct alternative is to use flower or grass seeds, which do not need to be cleaned up if tossed over a grassy area. Also, sparklers have become a popular send-off for the newlyweds. Another popular idea is using bubbles.

84. How much does wedding day transportation cost?
It can range from $35 to $100 per hour, depending on the type of transportation you choose. Many limousines are booked on a 3-hour minimum basis.

85. How much are parking fees?
Parking fees can range from $3 to $10 per car.

86. What should I do if I am having a wedding at home and there isn't enough room for our guests to park?
Find a nearby church or school where guests can park their cars. Then hire a shuttle service to take them to the house. Or you can hire a valet service to park guests' cars for them.

87. When should we register for gifts?
Four to six months before the wedding.

88. What kinds of things should we register for?
You should register for a variety of items in a broad price range so guests can make purchases within their budgets, or perhaps combine funds for a larger gift. While online registries are very easy, you want to make sure you choose at least one store that has brick-and-mortar locations so people who are not as Internet-savvy feel comfortable. You can register for anything from household appliances to electronics to charitable donations.

89. Can we ask for money instead of gifts?

Couples are getting married later in life these days, which means less need for a registry full of household appliances. If you want to ask for money, inform your wedding party members, who can spread the word to guests. Never ask for cash gifts on your invitations. Also, be aware that some guests will still want to get you a gift, so it's polite to create a small registry anyhow.

90. Who should I invite to my bridal shower?

Invite your close friends and the females in your fiancé's family. You may have several showers thrown for you, so be sure not to invite the same people to multiple showers (the exception being members of the wedding party, who may be invited to all showers without the obligation of bringing a gift). Only include people who have been invited to the wedding. The exception to this rule is a work shower, to which all coworkers may be invited, whether or not they are attending the wedding.

91. Does the groom attend the bridal shower?

It is becoming more popular to host showers with co-ed guest lists; however, he should skip any all-girls parties.

92. Can we have an after-party following the wedding reception?

An after-wedding party can mean inviting everyone to continue the party at a local lounge or bar, or reserving another part of your reception venue for late-night celebration. Although most older guests won't attend, you should still be polite and extend the invitation to everyone at the reception.

93. What is the day-after wedding brunch?

Many times the newlyweds will want to host a brunch the day after the wedding to spend one last bit of time with their guests and to thank them for coming to the wedding. This is especially true if many guests came from out of town or if you are having a destination wedding. Brunch can be much less formal than the rest of the wedding. Ask your family to help create this casual get-together by cooking or picking up brunch foods.

94. What is wedding insurance?

Wedding insurance protects couples planning a wedding from financial loss, due to unforeseen mishaps or cancellations on their wedding day. Because you can't plan for everything, you or your parents may want to consider purchasing some type of wedding insurance. Companies generally offer two types of wedding insurance products that can be purchased individually or as a package:

· Wedding Event Cancellation/Postponement Plus Insurance—protects your financial investment in your wedding; covers cancellation/postponement, lost deposits, and more

· Wedding Liability Insurance—protects you against financial liability arising from your wedding; required by many venues

95. **How much does wedding insurance cost?**

Wedding insurance—specifically cancellation/postponement insurance—is affordable and can provide great peace of mind. The cost should be about 1-2% of the amount of coverage—for example, a plan that provides $25,000 in coverage should cost about $300.

96. **If we are having a wedding at our home, do we need to purchase insurance to protect us in case of an accident during the wedding?**

Your homeowners insurance may already provide enough coverage for your wedding, but you should contact your provider to be absolutely sure. If you need additional coverage, you can purchase a liability policy from a wedding insurance provider, which is similar to what many venues have.

97. **When should we get our marriage license?**

Six to eight weeks before the wedding.

98. **How much does the marriage license cost?**

It depends upon the state where you live, but marriage licenses can cost anywhere from $20 to $100.

99. **What are the advantages of having a destination wedding?**

In recent years, destination weddings have enjoyed a tremendous growth in popularity. Couples are realizing that the time, effort and expense of planning a wedding and a honeymoon can be too much, and decide to combine them to create the perfect destination wedding. A five-day extended wedding weekend at a lovely beach resort can also be considerably cheaper than a reception and wedding for 200 guests at a luxury hotel in your preferred city or town. It is also a wonderful opportunity for friends and family to take a vacation while celebrating your happy union. These days, more brides and grooms are paying for their own weddings and finding it a huge expense. Then they must scale back on guest lists or skimp in other areas of the wedding, perhaps not ending up with the dream wedding they envisioned. You can save a considerable amount of money by having a destination wedding. It's also about quality time spent together, as you and your fiancé are surrounded by your closest friends and family, making it a wedding—and trip —to remember.

100. **How long is the average honeymoon?**

Eight days is the average for honeymoons, compared to 3 to 7 days for traditional vacations.

HONEYMOON

KAREN FRENCH

KAREN FRENCH

KAREN FRENCH

KAREN FRENCH

HONEYMOON

YOUR HONEYMOON IS THE TIME TO CELEBRATE your new life together as a married couple and fall even more in love. It will be the vacation of a lifetime. Deciding where to go and what to do is a process that can take several weeks or months. Go get started!

Maybe your idea of a perfect honeymoon is ten days of adventure, sightseeing and discovery, but for your fiancé, it may be ten days of resting in a beach chair and romantic strolls in the evening. The worksheets and checklists in this chapter will help you determine the ideal spot to visit for this amazing vacation, as well as how to budget, what to pack, and more.

There are many types of traditional and nontraditional honeymoons to consider. Laid-back tropical-island honeymoons are extremely popular, as are winter honeymoons in places like Canada and Alaska. Many couples also choose a honeymoon of dancing, gambling, and golf in Las Vegas.

Cruises are a very popular choice. You get to visit a wide variety of places in a short amount of time, and prices generally include almost every amenity, other than items like alcoholic beverages and spa treatments.

All-inclusive resorts are another great option that takes most of the guesswork out of pricing and budgeting. For one price, everything, from the rooms to meals to alcohol, is included. Most packages also include things like spa treatments, rounds of golf, and daily excursions and tours. Many resorts will provide special extras for honeymooners, including in-room jacuzzis, champagne, roses, massages, luxury bath products, and more.

Less traditional honeymoons that are growing in popularity include an African wildlife safari, camping, wine tasting in Italy, and eco-friendly trips to places like Costa Rica.

In this chapter, the Honeymoon Wish List will help you determine the type of weather, activities, accommodations, and amenities you and your fiancé imagine for your honeymoon. Each of you should place a check mark next to the items on the wish list that look most appealing. After you have finished, highlight those items that both of you feel are important (the items that you both checked), and you will have a great place to start planning.

Next, you need to create a budget based on your wish list. You want your honeymoon to be luxurious, romantic, and offer priceless memories, but you also want to create a reasonable budget. The average newlywed couple spends about $4,000 on their honeymoon. Some couples find that creating a honeymoon registry is a great way for friends and family to contribute to the trip. The "dollar dance" is another tradition. The bride and groom dance with their guests while accepting the dollar "dance fee" as a contribution to the honeymoon. Whatever you choose, planning and sticking to a budget ensures that you'll have a memorable and beautiful honeymoon without spending a fortune.

The table in this chapter lets you write down your general honeymoon budget, as well as what will be saved, acquired, and contributed. If you find that you are going over your budget, review your Honeymoon Wish List and eliminate a few lower priority items to free up some money for the most important ones. If you find you are under budget, celebrate with a special "gift" for yourselves (massages, a nice dinner, etc.).

Next, a tipping guide will help you determine the appropriate amounts to tip various service people on your honeymoon. Tipping customs vary from country to country. It is advisable to inquire about tipping with the international tourism board representing the country in which you'll be traveling. Some travel packages include gratuities in the total cost, some leave that to the guests, and some even discourage tipping (usually because they have built it into the total package price).

Lastly, a complete packing checklist ensures that you won't leave anything you need at home and that you'll be as comfortable as possible. Consider the change in climate of the location you'll be visiting. Also consider the temperatures of airplanes, trains, and boats.

Enjoy planning the honeymoon getaway you've always dreamed of!

Location	Bride	Groom
Hot Weather	✓	
Mild Weather		
Cold Weather		
Dry Climate		
Moist Climate	✓	
Beaches	✓	
Lakes		
Forests		
Mountains		
Fields	✓	
Sunsets		
Small Town		
Big City		
Popular Tourist Destination		
Visiting Among the Locals	✓	
Nighttime Weather Conducive to Outdoor Activities	✓	
Nighttime Weather Conducive to Indoor Activities		
"Modern" Resources and Services Available	✓	
"Roughing It" On Your Own		
Culture and Customs You Are Familiar and Comfortable With	✓ OR	
New Cultures and Customs You Would Like to Get to Know	✓	

Accommodations	Bride	Groom
All-Inclusive Resort Community		
Lodging with Families		
Lodging with Adults Only		
Lodging with Couples Only		
Lodging with Newlyweds Only		

HONEYMOON WISH LIST

Accommodations

Accommodations	Bride	Groom
Multi-Room Suite		
Champagne or Newlyweds Gifts in Room		
Minibar		
Flat-screen TV		
Fireplace in Room		
Balcony		
Private Jacuzzi in Room		
In-Room Massages		
Laundry Room on Premises		
Laundry/Dry Cleaning Services Available		
Bar/Lounge on Premises		
Spa on Premises		
Salon on Premises		
Gym on Premises		
Pool on Premises		
Poolside Bar		
Sauna or Hot Tub on Premises		
Fine Dining on Premises		

Meals

Meals	Bride	Groom
Casual Dining		
Formal Dining		
Fine Dining on Hotel Premises		
Prepared Yourself/Grocery Store		
Variety of Local and Regional Cuisine		
Traditional American Cuisine		
Opportunity for Picnics		
Exotic, International Menu		
Entertainment While Dining		

Meals	Bride	Groom
Set Meal Times		
Dining Based on Your Own Schedule		
Fast Food Restaurants		
Vegetarian/Special Diet Meals		
Delis, Diners		

Activities	Bride	Groom
Sunbathing		
Snorkeling		
Diving		
Swimming		
Jet Skiing		
Water Skiing		
Fishing		
Sailing		
Skiing/Snowboarding		
Hiking		
Rock Climbing		
Camping		
Golf		
Tennis		
Bike Riding		
Boating		
Bus/Guided Tours		
Walking Tours		
Historic Sites/Tours		
Sightseeing on Your Own		
Art Museums		
Theatre		

HONEYMOON WISH LIST

Nightlife

	Bride	Groom
Dancing		
Theatre/Shows		
Gambling/Casinos		
Bars/Pubs		
Nightclubs		
Wine Tasting		
Live Music		
Art Exhibitions		
Quiet Strolls		
Stargazing		
Relaxing in Front of a Fireplace		
Being Out with the Locals		
Being Out with Other Newlyweds		

Honeymoon Budget

Amount from the wedding budget set aside for the honeymoon	$
Amount groom is able to contribute from current funds/savings	$
Amount bride is able to contribute from current funds/savings	$
Amount to be saved/acquired by groom from now until the honeymoon date (monthly contributions, part-time job, gifts, bonuses)	$
Amount to be saved/acquired by bride from now until the honeymoon date (monthly contributions, part-time job, gifts, bonuses)	$
Amount from honeymoon registry and/or the "dollar dance"	$
Other contributions (family, etc.)	$
Budget Total Amount:	$

Air Travel
Skycaps .... $1 per bag
Flight Attendants .... None

Road Travel
Taxi Drivers .... 15% of fare (no less than 50 cents)
Limousine Driver 15%
Valet Parking $1
Tour Bus Guide $1

Rail Travel
Redcaps .... $1 per bag (or posted rate plus 50 cents)
Sleeping Car Attendant .... $1 per person
Train Conductor & Crew .... None
Dining Car Attendant ....15% of bill

Cruise
Cabin Steward .... $3 per person per day
Dining Room Waiter .... $3 per person per day
Busboy .... $1.50 per person per day
Maître D' .... At your discretion—recommended $10 - $20
Salon or Spa Personnel 15%
Bartender .... $1 - $2 per drink

Restaurants
Maître d', Head Waiter .... None (Unless special services provided, then typically $5)
Waiter/Waitress ....15% of bill (pretax total)
Bartender .... $1 - $2 per drink
Wine Steward ....15% of bill
Washroom Attendant .... $.50 - $1
Coat Check Attendant ....$1 per coat

Hotel/Resort
Concierge .... $2 - $10 for special attention or arrangements
Doorman .... $1 for hailing taxi
Bellhop ....$1 per bag + $1 for showing room
Room Service ....15% of bill
Chamber Maid .... $1 - $2 per day or $5 - $10 per week for longer stays
Pool Attendant ....$.50 for towel service

Miscellaneous
Barbershop .... 15% of cost
Beauty Salon .... 15% of cost
Manicure .... $1 - $5 depending on cost of service
Facial .... 15% of cost
Massage .... 15% of cost

HONEYMOON PACKING LIST

Travelers' first aid kit:

- ❏ Aspirin
- ❏ Antacid tablets
- ❏ Diarrhea medication
- ❏ Cold remedies/sinus decongestant
- ❏ Throat lozenges
- ❏ Antiseptic lotion
- ❏ Band-Aids
- ❏ Blister-prevention stick
- ❏ Breath mints
- ❏ Chapstick
- ❏ Insect repellent, insect bite medication
- ❏ Sunblock and sunburn relief lotion
- ❏ Lotion/hand cream
- ❏ Eye drops or eye lubricant
- ❏ Hand sanitizer
- ❏ Vitamins
- ❏ Birth control
- ❏ Physicians' names, addresses, and telephone numbers
- ❏ Names and phone numbers of people to contact in case of an emergency
- ❏ Health insurance phone numbers
  Note: Be sure to contact your provider to find out about coverage while traveling in the U.S. and abroad.
- ❏ Prescription drugs
  Note: These should be kept in their original pharmacy containers that provide both drug and doctor information. Be sure to note the drug's generic name. You will want to pack these in your carry-on baggage in case the bags you've checked are lost or delayed.

Packing checklist:
Carry-on Baggage

- ❏ Travelers' first aid kit
- ❏ Wallet (credit cards, traveler's checks)
- ❏ Jewelry and other sentimental and/or valuable items that you must bring
- ❏ Identification (passport, driver's license)
- ❏ Photocopies of the following important documents:
- ❏ Airline tickets
- ❏ Hotel/resort street address, phone number, written confirmation of arrangements and reservations
- ❏ Complete travel itinerary
- ❏ Name, address, and phone number of emergency contact person(s) back home
- ❏ Medicine prescriptions (including generic names) and eyeglass prescription information (or an extra pair), list of food and drug allergies
- ❏ Phone numbers (including after-hour emergency phone numbers) for health insurance company and personal physicians
- ❏ List of your traveler's checks' serial numbers and 24-hour phone number for reporting loss or theft
- ❏ Copy of your packing list. This will help you while packing up at the end of your trip. It will also be invaluable if a piece of your luggage gets lost, as you will know the contents that are missing.
- ❏ Phone numbers to the local U.S. embassy or consulate

☐ Warm sweater or jacket

☐ Any "essential" toiletries and makeup and one complete casual outfit in case checked baggage is delayed or lost

☐ Foreign language dictionary or translator

☐ Camera

☐ Maps and guide books

☐ Small bills/change (in U.S. dollars and in the appropriate foreign currency) for tipping

☐ Currency converter chart or calculator

☐ Reading material

☐ Music player or portable DVD player

☐ Eyeglasses

☐ Contact lenses

☐ Contact lens cleaner

☐ Sunglasses

☐ Kleenex, gum, breath mints, and any over-the-counter medicine to ease travel discomfort

☐ Neck pillow and blanket

☐ Address book and thank you notes (in case you have lots of traveling time)

☐ This book

☐ Your budget sheet

Checked baggage:

Clothing: *Consider the total number of each clothing item you will need.*

Casual Wear:

☐ Shorts

☐ Pants

☐ Tops

☐ Jackets/sweaters

☐ Sweatshirts/sweatsuits

☐ Belts

☐ Socks

☐ Underwear/panties & bras

☐ Walking shoes/sandals/flip-flops

Athletic Wear:

☐ Shorts

☐ Sweatpants

☐ Tops

☐ Sweatshirts/jackets

☐ Swimsuits, swimsuit cover-up

☐ Aerobic activity outfit

☐ Athletic equipment

☐ Socks

☐ Underwear/panties & exercise bras

☐ Running/hiking shoes

Evening Wear:

☐ Pants/skirts/dresses

☐ Belts

☐ Dress shirts/blouses

☐ Sweaters

☐ Jackets/blazers/ties

☐ Socks or pantyhose/slips

☐ Underwear/panties & bras

HONEYMOON PACKING LIST

- ❏ Accessories/jewelry
- ❏ Shoes/heels
- ❏ Pajamas
- ❏ Lingerie
- ❏ Slippers
- ❏ Robe

Formal Wear:
- ❏ Dress pants/suits/tuxedo
- ❏ Dresses/gowns
- ❏ Accessories/jewelry
- ❏ Socks or pantyhose/slips
- ❏ Underwear/panties & bras
- ❏ Dress shoes/heels

Miscellaneous items:
- ❏ An additional set of the important document photocopies as packed in your carry-on bag
- ❏ Travel tour books, tourism bureau information numbers
- ❏ Journal
- ❏ Special honeymoon gift for your new spouse
- ❏ Any romantic items or favorite accessories
- ❏ Camera and phone chargers
- ❏ Plastic bags for dirty laundry
- ❏ Large plastic or nylon tote bag for bringing home new purchases
- ❏ Small sewing kit and safety pins
- ❏ Hair-styling tools
- ❏ Travel iron, lint brush

- ❏ Compact umbrella, fold-up rain slickers
- ❏ Travel alarm clock
- ❏ Video camera

For International travel:
- ❏ Passports/visas
- ❏ Electric converters and adapter plugs
- ❏ Copy of appropriate forms showing proof of required vaccinations/inoculations

Items to leave behind:
(with a trusted contact person)
- ❏ Photocopy of all travel details (complete itineraries, names, addresses, and telephone numbers)
- ❏ Photocopy of credit cards along with 24-hour telephone number to report loss or theft. (Be sure to also get the number to call when traveling abroad. It will be a different number than their U.S. 1-800 number.)
- ❏ Photocopy of traveler's checks with 24-hour phone number to report loss or theft
- ❏ Photocopy of passport identification page, along with date and place of issue
- ❏ Photocopy of driver's license
- ❏ Any irreplaceable items